SHAPING HISTORY

The University of Alabama Huntsville Foundation

By

Michael D. Ward

© 2008 The University of Alabama Huntsville Foundation

AuthorHouse™
1663 Liberty Drive, Suite 200
Bloomington, IN 47403
www.authorhouse.com
Phone: 1-800-839-8640

© 2009 Michael D. Ward

No part of this book may be reproduced, stored in a retrieval system, or
transmitted by any means without the written permission of the author.

First published by AuthorHouse 1/19/08

ISBN: 978-1-4389-4468-5 (sc)
ISBN: 978-1-4389-4467-8 (dj)

Library of Congress Control Number 2008912037

Printed in the United States of America
Bloomington, Indiana

This book is printed on acid-free paper.

Patrick W. Richardson

Dedication

This book is dedicated to the memory of Patrick W. Richardson, known fondly as the "Father of The University of Alabama in Huntsville." At a meeting of the University of Alabama Huntsville Foundation, Pat, as he was known, introduced a request that the foundation engage Mike Ward to write a history of the foundation. This request was warmly received and passed without dissent. He died shortly thereafter, leaving big shoes to fill in his devoted support and advancement of UAH.

To honor Pat, the University reserved the license plate UAH001 for him. He drove his Lincoln with it proudly displayed until his death. After his death, his wife, Mary, gave this University vanity plate to UAH. It was placed in the Huntsville time capsule as a fitting reminder that Pat was, indeed, the father of UAH and he was number one in the hearts of his fellow members of the UAH Foundation.

TABLE OF CONTENTS

Introduction

The pages that follow chronicle the creation, evolution, and multifaceted impact of the University of Alabama Huntsville Foundation (UAHF). They trace the growth of the city of Huntsville and the area surrounding it as an internationally acclaimed center for research and development in science, engineering, and technology. They describe the concurrent evolution of The University of Alabama in Huntsville (UAH) as the pre-eminent academic center in Alabama for research in engineering, physical science, environmental science, and computational science. They recount the seminal contributions that the UAH Foundation, and the outstanding men and women who have constituted its members, has made in helping to make some very good things to happen in Huntsville, Alabama.

The UAHF is a rarity among university-related foundations in that the UAHF existed even before the university it now serves was created. The chapters that follow detail how Huntsville leaders came together to form the predecessor of the UAHF as a land-holding operation supporting the orderly development of Cummings Research Park, of which UAH occupies the easternmost extremity. Later chapters describe how the UAHF gradually took on greater and greater responsibility for the support of UAH itself, becoming, ultimately, UAH's independent, university-related foundation.

From its inception, the UAH Foundation has captured the attention and support of many of Huntsville's leading citizens. Descriptions of the individual members of the original Foundation are presented as an Appendix to this history; a list of all past and present members is also provided. These men and women have brought independent wisdom, insight, critique, and advice to the operation of the University. They have brought substantial financial support as well.

Indeed, the UAHF and its members have supplied continuing support, and made crucial investments in UAH at particularly critical times in UAH's history.

The Foundation provided more than a million dollars to secure expert legal assistance when the University's very existence was being challenged in a long-lasting Title VI lawsuit.

The Foundation has provided hundreds of thousands of dollars annually for scholarships for outstanding students from local area high schools, and for unrestricted support for University academic and athletic programs.

The Foundation underwrote part of the cost of UAH's first residence hall, and of its second, and of its third, assisted by a million-dollar gift by Foundation member John Hendricks.

Mrs. Susie Hudson, wife of Foundation member Jim Hudson, gave more than a million dollars to assist in the development of UAH's Fraternity and Sorority Row. Foundation member Mark Smith and Foundation member-to-be Linda Smith made a similar gift in support of the project.

Foundation member Olin King arranged a multi-million dollar gift/purchase of a 140,000 sq. ft. building from the then SCI Corporation to UAH to ultimately yield the facility now known as Olin B. King Technology Hall. Foundation member Gene Sapp later helped the University to acquire an additional structure and additional adjacent land through a subsequent gift/purchase. Mr. King also contributed $2 million of the value of the UAH building now known as Shelbie King Hall.

Foundation member Tony Chan and Foundation member-to-be Kathy Chan have had a long history of providing UAH with grants from the Pei Ling Chan Trust, as well as personal gifts, that are in excess of a million dollars.

Foundation member Robert Heath contributed more than three million dollars toward the gift/purchase of the facility that became the original core of the National Space Science and Technology Center and the Robert (Bud) Cramer Research Hall.

The UAH Foundation and its members contribute far more than financial support to UAH. They bring expertise, experience, and advice on matters of common concern and interest. They help to develop understanding and appreciation for UAH within the community at large, and with officials at local, state, and federal levels. They are among the University's prime advocates and most persuasive ambassadors. They have played key roles in helping to create the highly regarded, highly diverse, student-friendly, research-intensive university that UAH now has become. Their continued support promises an even brighter UAH future. This document is a testament to the vision, dedication, and generosity of the leadership and members of the UAH Foundation and the many signal UAH successes they have helped to create.

Frank Franz
President, UAH, 1991-2007
President Emeritus, Professor of Physics Emeritus

Prologue

In every community's history, there are moments and choices that forever shape its future. For some communities, those choices have been ruinous, relegating them to dismal fortunes that seem to inextricably spiral downward.

For other communities, luck and good judgment have created opportunities that bear unlikely fruit and set new directions. Huntsville, Alabama found itself at a crossroad mid-way through the last century, when opportunity knocked hard at its front door.

In 1949, Huntsville was the thirteenth largest Alabama city, outranked by Birmingham, Mobile, Montgomery, Anniston, Selma, Gadsden, Dothan, Florence, Decatur, Phenix City, and Tuscaloosa. Madison County was the seventh most populous Alabama county, behind Jefferson, Mobile, Montgomery, Calhoun, Etowah, and Tuscaloosa Counties. The city's population stood at 16,406; the county's at 73,032.

Huntsville and Madison County's economies were unspectacular in perhaps every regard. Its surviving cotton mills were marginally performing. The end of World War II had prompted the closure of the area's largest employer, one of Huntsville's two U.S. Army Arsenals.

Fast forward to 2005: Huntsville's population outstrips all but three other Alabama cities and Madison County's population ranks third. In terms of "place of employment" Madison County ranks behind only Jefferson County in the state.

Why has Huntsville prospered as other Alabama communities have seen their fortunes stall or decline?

To be sure, Huntsville was dealt some very lucky and unlikely cards. The fateful decisions to locate two U.S. Army Arsenals in Madison County in 1941 were certainly future-altering opportunities, not entirely within the control of local leaders. Undoubtedly, though, other communities faced with similar fortunes on the eve of the United States' entry into WWII have not enjoyed such follow-on success.

Community leadership and vision have proved to be the magic ingredients propelling Huntsville's growth. The inspired decisions by a relatively small group of people, beginning in the mid-1940s, transcended the good fortune of having the Arsenals in Madison County.

This is the story of a group of community leaders who made critical choices through a variety of related and unrelated organizations and helped change Huntsville's fortune.

The names of these leaders are perhaps not as well known as they should be. The organizations through which they worked and their histories are all but unknown today. Men like Patrick Richardson, Carl T. Jones, George Mahoney, Charles Shaver, Louis Salmon, Beirne Spragins, Robert K. "Buster" Bell, Tom Thrasher, Kenneth Noojin, and Vance Thornton provided the inspired leadership at critical moments.

Key partner organizations included the local Chamber of Commerce, the Huntsville Industrial Expansion Committee, the City of Huntsville, and Huntsville Industrial Sites. Later, those efforts included the University of Alabama and the University of Alabama in Huntsville. At the heart of accelerating Huntsville's growth were the University of Alabama Huntsville Foundation and its predecessor organizations.

The middle of the last century was a period of great change for a community that had seen very little change for the previous 100 years. Like much of the rest of the South, the foundations of Huntsville's economy were based largely on the meager living that its people could scratch from the earth and earn at the local textile mills.

Huntsville had been among the leading cotton-producing and milling communities in the southern United States in the 19th century.

Manufacturing was dominated by the textile mills that first located out in the County in the early 1800s. Later, in the 1930s, Huntsville would boast of being the "Watercress Capital of the World," a tribute perhaps more to the marketing skills of the exotic industry than the economic impact that cress had on the region.

As the decade of the 1940s was drawing to an end, only three of the area's nine cotton mills were still operating. The Huntsville Arsenal, one of the two WWII arsenals located in Madison County, had been closed and declared surplus by the federal government. Virtually all of the 11,000-15,000 people who had worked there making chemical munitions during the years of the war effort had lost their jobs.

Against this bleak backdrop, two unrelated but very important opportunities emerged. In 1949, the Army decided to use the arsenals' nearly 40,000 acres for its rocket research program and to relocate the German V2 rocket team from Fort Bliss, Texas. The second significant decision would come just a couple of weeks later when the University of Alabama announced plans to open an extension office in Huntsville. Both decisions would be implemented in 1950.

Ultimately these two unrelated events would create a demand for an institution of higher education and, as businesses interest in the region heightened, a demand for ready industrial property on which businesses could locate their operations. Those two interests would later find common ground in the University of Alabama Huntsville Foundation.

Luck, timing, perseverance, hard work, political muscle, and a healthy concern about the community's future ultimately would carry the day for Huntsville.

Chapter One: Sowing The Seeds Of A University

Living in a community with an economy rooted in agriculture and the low-tech textile industry, the average Huntsvillian didn't have much use for higher education for the first 145 years of the city's history. Mid-way through the twentieth century a quarter of the city's population had fewer than five years of formal schooling; less than a fifth had finished high school; and college graduates were almost as scarce as hen's teeth.[1] Those who did seek more than a grade-school education typically went to universities in Tuscaloosa, Auburn or beyond the state's borders.

Huntsville enjoyed a brief and wholly unsuccessful flirtation with higher education in 1935 when the University of Alabama considered it as a potential site for university classes. Those plans fizzled from a lack of community interest without the first class ever having been taught.

In 1937, Huntsville's larger neighbor to the west, Decatur, enjoyed only a slightly more successful, albeit brief, venture into higher education when the University of Alabama offered classes there for a year. But that effort, too, failed.

It wasn't until 1946 that interest in establishing a local campus for higher education began to gain a foothold in Huntsville. That year, two things happened "almost contemporaneously," according to Huntsville native and then-University of Alabama Law School student Patrick W. Richardson.[2]

That year, the U.S. Chamber of Commerce issued a study ranking education as the number one factor influencing economic growth, "showing figures like per capita income, bank deposits, the number of telephones, and magazine subscriptions," noted Richardson, who was at the time a graduate fellow teaching in the UA College of Commerce.[3] About the same time, the University's Extension Division announced plans to open a branch center in Gadsden. "I felt that if they could have one in Gadsden, we could have one in Huntsville," Richardson added.[4]

In 1947, Richardson and fellow University of Alabama law student Macon Weaver suggested to L. H. Pinkston, secretary of the Huntsville Chamber of Commerce, that his organization explore the possibility of establishing a University branch office in Huntsville.[5] In order to acquaint the Chamber of Commerce with the University Extension program, Richardson arranged a meeting of the Chamber with Extension Division officials.[6] It and subsequent meetings would prove of critical importance.

Richardson and Weaver first visited Dr. Richard Eastwood in the University's Extension Division. "After several meetings with Dick Eastwood, he apparently became convinced that the only way to get rid of me was to pass me along to someone else," Richardson said. "That person was Dr. John R. Morton, who was director of Adult Education."[7]

On July 27, 1947, Dr. Morton, the Extension Division's director of Continuous Education, met with local officials to describe the purpose and basic requirements of operating an Extension Center. A center would offer local high school graduates and adults the opportunity to complete two years of accredited college work without leaving Huntsville. The University of Alabama would provide the school administration and faculty supervision; it was the community's responsibility to supply classroom space near the downtown area and a minimum of 200 students.[8]

Little headway was made in 1948, but the effort began to gain momentum the next year when the lobbying efforts took some highly public steps. "I guess Jack Morton finally became convinced that the only way he was going to get rid of me was to tell me that if I could prove [its feasibility], he would do it. So I came home to prove it, 'it' being that Huntsville could support a University center, that there was a need and a market." [9]

Concurrent and coincidental efforts by Reese T. Amis, editor of *The Huntsville Times,* to relocate Snead Junior College in Boaz and/or Athens College to the community were mounted, though an editorial campaign failed to gain traction. That effort had, however, drawn the attention of a core group of community leaders who were convinced of the value of bringing higher education to town.

"I went to Reese Amis," said Richardson, "and persuaded him that there was a realistic possibility of getting a University Center established here, that I had a commitment from Dr. Morton that if I could demonstrate a demand for it, he would recommend to the dean of the Extension Division that they open one." [10]

The University of Alabama representatives were skeptical that there was sufficient interest to sustain the effort. The Chamber established a University Center Committee, and Richardson was selected as the obvious choice to head it. Serving with him on the panel were Reese Amis, Vance Thornton, real estate agent and member of the City Council; Dr. Harvey Nelson, superintendent of Huntsville City Schools; Edward Anderson, superintendent of Madison County Schools; Frank Rice, Edward Burwell, Jr., A.W. Burkett, Will Dickson, and Schuyler Richardson, who were representatives of various local veterans groups.[11]

"The veterans were coming home from the war and they were all unemployed," Richardson said. "The best deal going for them was the G.I. Bill, which really accounted for the demand for the University Center." [12]

The committee visited local high schools, industries and veterans organizations to generate support. The Extension Division sent materials to the Chamber, which, in turn, passed them along to local businesses, asking what courses the center should offer if it were opened in January of 1950.[13]

"Late in the buildup of the series *The Times* published a story about the University Center, with a coupon to fill out, clip and send in if you thought you might be interested in attending classes at a university center. We got enough of those coupons returned – 499 of them – to convince Dr. Morton that the demand was there," Richardson said in a 2001 interview. "He was very skeptical of my numbers. I had to take the coupons to him so he could see them." Richardson and the local committee met with Morton September 21, 1949 and presented the data.

Headlines on the front page of *The Huntsville Times* the next day declared, "January Date is Indicated on New Center." The story went on to describe Morton's favorable impression of the local cooperative effort, including the questionnaires and letters of support from officials at Redstone Arsenal, Huntsville Manufacturing

Company, General Shoe Company, Martin Stamping and Stove Company, and Solvay Process Co. officials.

Dr. Morton suggested that a center might be opened as early as November of 1949 if placed under the direction of the Gadsden Center, but the local committee rejected that offer.[14]

Encouraged nonetheless by the meeting, Richardson sent a letter to Dr. John M. Gallalee, president of the University of Alabama, citing the great need for and local interest in a center and the great amount of time invested in the effort by Drs. Morton, Lee Bidgood, and R.E. Tidwell. Richardson invited Dr. Gallalee to Huntsville to talk with the Chamber committee.[15]

A date was finally set for a meeting on November 15, 1949 with Drs. Gallalee and Tidwell, the latter the dean of the University Extension Division. The Huntsville committee sent invitations to "60 civic leaders, city councilmen, county commissioners, and industrial executives, members of the Madison County legislative delegation as well as legislators from Marshall, Jackson and Limestone counties. Both Edward Anderson, Madison County schools superintendent, and Dr. Harvey D. Nelson, Huntsville school[s] superintendent and both school boards will also attend."[16]

The Huntsville Times story preceding the meeting quoted Richardson as saying, "The campaign for a University of Alabama extension center here is not an ordinary civic drive, but a matter vitally important to the future welfare of Madison County boys and girls." Richardson continued, "The project will succeed or fail, once and for all, according to the attendance and interest shown in the Tuesday conference with President Gallalee and Dean Tidwell."

The November 15 meeting was held in the City Electric System auditorium. By newspaper account it was attended by a "large crowd of Huntsville, Madison County and North Alabama residents who jammed the auditorium."

At that meeting, Dr. Gallalee announced that classes for the University Center would start on January 15, 1950 and that the West Huntsville High School was the most likely site.

With that announcement, the three-year campaign to locate the University Center that would one day become UAH had triumphed. It had been a busy month for Huntsville.

Just two weeks before this announcement, big news had come. It concerned the future of Redstone Arsenal.

Chapter Two: The Arsenal Alters A Region's Direction

Fire trucks delivered the special edition of the July 3, 1941 *Huntsville Times* proclaiming in banner headlines the Army's decision to locate an arsenal in Madison County. Some $40-million would be invested in facilities and thousands of people would be employed. The news was heaven-sent for a struggling mill-village town down on its luck.

It was the eve of the United States' entry into WWII, just months before the Japanese would bomb Pearl Harbor. War planning, however, was obviously already well underway. Huntsville was strategically located some 350 miles from the Gulf Coast, placing it just outside the bombing range of an aircraft carrier-launched assault. It was also located near a river and on a railroad line giving it access to key transportation systems to help move large supplies of munitions. Still another advantage to this North Alabama site was the ready proximity of nitrate mines in the Shoals region of North Alabama – nitrates being one of the primary ingredients of explosives. Funding for what would become the Huntsville Arsenal, the nation's second chemical manufacturing and storage facility, had been approved in April 1941.

According to news reports twenty-plus years later, the true beginning of what became the Redstone complex had occurred about two months before the July 3 headlines. Then-Chamber President (volunteer) George Mahoney (pronounced Man-ney) received a call at his clothing store (Johnson and Mahoney) from Mr. James Center of Nashville, industrial agent for the old Nashville, Chattanooga & St. Louis Railway. Center said he had wind of a proposed industrial development that might possibly be located at Huntsville and that the following day he was bringing in a group of people connected with the project to look over an area of Madison County. It was acreage where the NC&St.L had, not so coincidentally, a long and rather idle line of track running south all the way to the Tennessee River.

Mahoney recalled that Center asked him to select a friend who knew land values in the area and have the two of them join the visitors. Mahoney asked Lawrence Goldsmith if he would come along; Goldsmith, a local businessman, consented. Center and the two Huntsville businessmen the next day showed the mysterious visitors (including, it later turned out, a U.S. Army lieutenant colonel who had worn civilian clothes, and an Army project engineer) around the land they had come to see and answered their questions about real estate prices and various facets of the community itself.

When the party had gone, Mahoney and Goldsmith, still without much solid information to go on, wired U.S. Sen. Lister Hill and then-U.S. Representative John Sparkman in Washington, advising them to investigate and seek to land this thing – whatever it was – for Huntsville.

Mahoney gave full credit to James Center for placing Huntsville's name firmly in the hat as a site for the facility that has since brought worldwide fame – as well as fortune – to the city and region. "The first indication we in Huntsville had that anything at all was brewing was from Mr. Center," he said. It was later rumored that at the time Center entered the picture as Huntsville's advocate, the proposed new chemical arsenal was all but "in the bag" for Pine Bluff, Arkansas.[17]

Also working to Redstone's advantage was the Deep South political powerhouse of then-Congressman Sparkman and U.S. Senators Lister Hill and Tom Heflin of Alabama.

On June 8, 1941, the first stop on the Army's inspection tour for a new chemical manufacturing and storage facility site was made at Huntsville. Official accounts note the inspection team was escorted initially to a spot on the southern side of the Tennessee River. After this location was rejected as unsuitable for building without excessive leveling, the Army team looked at an alternate site on the southwestern edge of the city, on the river's northern bank.

Later that month, the chief of the Army's Chemical Warfare Service (CWS) wrote a letter suggesting that additional facilities for the

CWS be located near Huntsville. The letter outlined the plant requirements and requested authorization and necessary funds to acquire the land and equipment, as well as provide for construction.

Ultimately, the U.S. Army would locate two adjacent arsenals at a cost of more than $85 million on 40,000 acres in Madison County.[18] Redstone Ordnance Plant, drawing its name from the region's red clay soil that had sustained the area's agricultural base, would be built next to Huntsville Arsenal to capitalize on the enormous economy of locating an Ordnance Corps shell-loading/assembly plant close to the Huntsville Chemical Warfare manufacturing facility. The Ordnance site was renamed Redstone Arsenal in 1943.

Development of the facilities and hiring started at what would certainly be considered breakneck speed today. Civil service hiring began a mere nine days after the first Arsenal public announcement, and construction contracts were awarded a couple of weeks later.

By the time the Japanese had dropped their bombs on Pearl Harbor, the first buildings at the Arsenal had already been completed and more than 75 miles of railroad track had been laid.

Early workforce plans called for the employment of women in the event that "man"-power became scarce. Arrangements were made with the Civil Service Commission, which soon announced job examinations for female trainees. At the time, the use of women in a factory environment was clearly frowned upon, but subsequent events made these moves appear to have been clairvoyant. By December 1942, about 40 percent of Redstone production-line employees were women.[19]

Huntsville Arsenal's first production facility was activated in March of 1942. The items produced there included colored smoke grenades, and the dye used in them colored the workers' clothing and stained their skin. Reportedly it was not uncommon to see people of rainbow hues out and about in the Huntsville area. The Arsenal also produced mass quantities of gel-type incendiaries.

During WWII more than 27 million items of chemical munitions, with a total value of more than $134.5 million, were produced at Huntsville Arsenal. Personnel there were frequently recognized for their outstanding record in the production of war materiel. During the war, more than 45.2 million units of ammunition were loaded and assembled at what had become the consolidated Redstone.

At their peak in 1945, the combined Arsenals employed more than 11,000 workers. Huntsville Arsenal's civil service employees peaked at 6,707 and Redstone Arsenal's at 4,400. The Arsenals employed a relatively small number of uniformed military, peaking at Huntsville Arsenal with 580 in October of 1942.

But as quickly as the jobs had come, they vanished once the war ended in August of 1945. In June of 1945, the first reduction-in-force (RIF) had been implemented at Redstone Arsenal. On August 17, 1945, production at Redstone essentially ceased, although some lines operated a while for part of the day to complete items already in process. During the last quarter of 1945, not a single item was manufactured or assembled at Redstone.

At the end of WWII, Huntsville was known chiefly as the largest cotton market east of Memphis. It had 3,500 homes, three large cotton mills and nine small industries.[20]

Efforts in the mid-to-late 1940s to attract private industry to the vacant Arsenal facilities were largely unsuccessful, although the business community was very active in its marketing efforts. In August of 1947, a building formerly used to manufacture gas masks was leased to Keller Motors Corporation (originally the Dixie Motor Car Corporation). The plant was to be used for manufacturing, assembling, testing, and selling automobiles and related products. Unfortunately Keller Motors would fold after its namesake George Keller died suddenly of a heart attack on the eve of the company's successful stock sale in 1949, never putting its "woodie" station-wagon automobile into production.

In 1947, Huntsville Arsenal was declared excess and the process for disposing of the property was begun. Redstone Arsenal, on the other hand, found the glimmer of new life in 1948 when the Chief of Ordnance designated it as the Army's future center of research and development activities in the field of rockets and related weaponry. The Arsenal was officially reactivated as the site of the Ordnance Rocket Center on June 1, 1949.

Huntsville Arsenal property was slated to be either sold or returned to the previous owners on several dates in 1949. As each deadline approached, however, the sale would be postponed as senior Pentagon planners considered other potential uses for the facilities.

In April of 1949, both Thiokol and Rohm and Haas signed contracts to do research and development work on rockets, rocket propellants and jet propulsion at Redstone Arsenal.

About the same time, community promoters learned of the Air Force's interest in developing an aerodynamics wind tunnel R&D center and went to work to bring the operation to Redstone/Huntsville Arsenal. No-holds-barred political battles ensued. Ultimately the major wind tunnel facility went to a site near Tullahoma, Tennessee, 59 miles to Huntsville's north. It became the Arnold Engineering Development Center. The North Alabama community was bruised at the end of the effort.

Following the Air Force's March 17, 1949 decision to pass on the Huntsville Arsenal site, the Army directed that the post be advertised for sale by July 1, 1949. Bid opening was set for September 30, 1949. But the sale never took place. The Army found it needed this land for the new mission developing at Redstone.

Colonel Holger N. "Ludy" Toftoy, the head of the Army's guided missile efforts, had gotten word in August of 1949 that his request for expanded facilities at Fort Bliss, near El Paso, Texas, had been denied. Toftoy was the Army visionary who had brought the nucleus of the German V2 team to the U.S. in an effort codenamed "Project Paperclip" at the end of WWII.

More of the Texas base was now needed for the threatened Korean conflict. "The Army also saw an urgent need for a ballistic rocket missile, and asked the former German rocket team 'Peenemuenders' to develop a missile similar to the V2 as quickly as possible."[21]

Two weeks later, Toftoy visited North Alabama to check out the mothballed Huntsville Arsenal. Impressed with what he saw, Colonel Toftoy had several members of the rocket team visit the Tennessee Valley site.

The Huntsville Times on September 16, 1949, reported that "Ft. Bliss Rocket Group At Arsenal." The story went on to report:

> Major James P. Hamill and 13 members of his staff
> of officers, engineers and scientists from the

Ordnance Research and Development Division Suboffice (Rocket), Ft. Bliss Texas are visiting Redstone arsenal for the purpose of conferring on the problems connected with the rocket research and development program now under way at the arsenal.

The group arrived Wednesday afternoon by Army airplane direct from Ft. Bliss and is planning to depart Saturday morning.

Conferences are including complete inspections of all facilities for the continuation and expansion of the general rocket research and development activities.

Accompanying Major Hamill are Captain Lorenzo A. Mella, Captain James C. Miller, Captain Joseph B. Sestito, Warrant Officer Fred Guenthner, Warrant Officer John J. Lockwood, Master Sergeant Appler, James Fagan, Professor Theodor Buchhold, Hannes Leuhrsen, Dr. Josef Michel, Eberhard Rees, Ludwig Roth, Dr. Martin Schilling and professor [Wernher] von Braun.

The last seven persons named are civilian scientists who are assisting the Ordnance department in advanced rocket research and development work.

Attracted by the relatively new facilities and lush green rolling mountains surrounding the Arsenal, Dr. von Braun quickly embraced the new Huntsville site. Recalling von Braun's reconnaissance trip report, Dorette Kersten Schlidt, a von Braun secretary at the wartime German rocket R&D base at Peenemuende and later at Ft. Bliss, said that von Braun excitedly told his German compatriots: "Oh, it looks like home! So green, green, everything is so green, with mountains all around!"[22]

Encouraged by all the favorable reports, Colonel Toftoy personally petitioned the Army Vice Chief of Staff, General Matthew Ridgeway, to relocate the team to the Huntsville/Redstone Arsenal site. Spreading out a large map of the Arsenal on the floor of Ridgeway's office, Toftoy discovered that his pointer wasn't long enough and so he proceeded to crawl around on the floor to point out the many splendid attributes that this site offered. As he concluded his plea for the Redstone site, Toftoy found himself at General Ridgeway's feet and looking up said, "General Ridgeway, I'm on my hands and knees here, literally and figuratively, begging you for this place."

On October 28, 1949, the Secretary of the Army approved the transfer of the Fort Bliss rocket team to Redstone Arsenal, including the German rocket scientist team that had been working at first in secret there.

Banner *Huntsville Times* headlines on November 14, 1949 trumpeted the Army's decision: "Fort Bliss, Texas, Rocket Office To Be Moved To Redstone Arsenal." Coincidentally, this announcement would precede the University of Alabama's decision to locate an Extension Center in Huntsville by less than two weeks.

In the days that followed the Army's announcement, it was only natural for the rank-and-file citizens of the Huntsville area to anticipate a hiring surge similar to the employment rush of the 1941 Arsenal announcement. But this new direction for the Arsenal would not initially bring the thousands of relatively low-skilled jobs that the munitions production lines had offered.

With the arrival of the Fort Bliss group beginning April 15, 1950, Redstone Arsenal officially entered the missile era. Apparently it did not strike anyone as being overly odd that the Germans leading the rocket program would be occupying property on the Arsenal that only five years before had held more than 1,000 German prisoners of war.

The relocation of the 500-person rocket team from Fort Bliss had caused a sudden and dramatic surge in housing demand, badly stretching an already tight residential market. Initially, many of those who had been transferred from Fort Bliss were housed in barracks on the base. A Chamber of Commerce advisory committee was established to help address the issue.

The decade of the 1940s had wrought phenomenal change for Huntsville, and the underpinnings of the region's future growth were in place. Like a phoenix, the Arsenal had found new life.

Chapter Three: The Foundation Sinks Its Roots

In 1940, Huntsville's corporate city limits included just a few square miles around the area that is today known as downtown. The unofficial hub of activity for the leaders of the business community was the men's clothing store "Johnson and Mahoney," located on Clinton Street in downtown. Proprietor George Mahoney was one of the leading business community activists, serving as President of the Chamber of Commerce in 1938 and 1939.

After getting a cup of coffee at the Central Café two doors away on the corner, businessmen would gather in the clothing store to discuss the concerns of the day and most importantly, to make their collective plans as community leaders.

There, among the fedoras, suits and wing-tips, an important topic of conversation in the mid-1940s, even before World War II had ended and the Arsenal's employment rolls had begun to shrink, was the inevitable military downsizing that lay ahead. The imperative was clear: Something must be done to prepare the community for the hard times ahead.

The principal economic development organization at the time for Huntsville and Madison County was the Chamber of Commerce. Here in the mid-1940s was a growing realization that the community needed a new organization focused on the relatively fresh enterprise of industrial recruitment. This awareness became the motivating force behind the creation in 1944 of the Huntsville Industrial Expansion Committee (HIEC). Although the HIEC shared office space in the same building with the Chamber, each entity maintained separate organizational structures and funding.

While the Chamber handled traditional civic-building responsibilities, the HIEC became the aggressive industrial recruiting arm of the community's economic development efforts. Its founders included many of the same people who would later establish the organizations upon which the UAH Foundation would be built. Not coincidentally, many of those same men occupied offices near Johnson and Mahoney's haberdashery.

At the time of its founding in the mid-1940s, the HIEC group believed that federal spending on defense programs would one day decline and that the economic health of the region depended upon diversification of its economic base. [23] Adding to the locals' concern, the city of Decatur had recently landed the regional economic development office for the Tennessee Valley Authority, causing Huntsville business leaders to fear development might be steered away from the city.[24]

The following is a first-hand report by George Mahoney of the founding of the Huntsville Industrial Expansion Committee[25]:

A public spirited group of businessmen realizing the necessity of bringing new industry into our community organized the Huntsville Industrial Expansion Committee of the Chamber of Commerce.

On September 7, 1944, the following men, Karl Woltersdorf, Lawrence Goldsmith, M.B. Spragins, Reese T. Amis, F. H. Thomas, and George M. Mahoney, met with Mr. Fitzgerald Hall, President of the N.C. & St. Louis Railroad, Mr. Brownlee Curley, industrialist from Nashville, Tennessee and Mr. Robert Strickland, president of the Trust Company of Atlanta. This was a breakfast meeting given by Mr. Hall on his private car near the N.C. & St. L. depot. The committee present heard the many helpful suggestions of the three visiting gentlemen and the outcome of this meeting was the formation of the Huntsville Industrial Expansion Committee.

A meeting was held on September 11th at which time about 100 businessmen were called together to officially organize the Huntsville Industrial Expansion Committee, nominate officers, and to adopt a constitution and by-laws for the new organization.

On September 19th, another meeting was held at which time a goal of $25,000 was set to be raised by public subscriptions. George Mahoney was elected president; M. B. Spragins, vice-president; L. B. Goldsmith, treasurer, and F. H. Thomas, secretary. Other directors were Karl Wolterdorf, F. N. Sefton, C. J. Mock, Percy Noble, J. F. Chambers, H. E. Monroe, C. B. Ragland, K.E. Thomas, Charles E. Shaver, F. H. Ford, Earnest White, W. O. Mason, Dr. E. V. Caldwell, and Edward McGregor.

A number of other meetings were held at which time a Fund Chairman and other Chairmen were appointed. One of the important committees, the Brochure Committee, produced, through their effort, a very attractive booklet pertaining to the many advantages of locating industry in Madison County.

Solicitations of funds began shortly after the meeting of September 19th and the goal of $25,000 was subscribed.

Unique in its composition is the Huntsville Industrial Expansion Committee, since the funds raised could only be used for promotion, entertainment and travel.

No funds could be used for the purchase of sites or other physical properties.

On June 12, 1945, Mahoney, then chairman of the HIEC, addressed the Huntsville Rotary Club and outlined the need for aggressive local economic development efforts. According to Mahoney, the HIEC was organized under the Chamber of Commerce and was working to secure the best advice from the country's leading industrial chiefs and economic experts. The committee scored some early economic development successes, locating the General Shoe Company and John Blue Manufacturing to Huntsville in the late 1940s.[26]

In 1947, the HIEC produced a 63-page industrial recruiting booklet proclaiming Huntsville's many fine attributes and touting the ready supply of available former Redstone workers. "An estimated 90 percent of this tried and tested personnel are still on the scene – most of it going back to its farm and city homes in the area. It is available for Huntsville's new industries."[27]

About this time, another important organization, the Army Advisory Committee, was established by Redstone to provide critical lines of communications between the Arsenal and community leaders. Early members of the Advisory Committee included a soon-to-become-familiar lineup of local leaders: Huntsville Mayor "Spec" Searcy, George Mahoney, Roy Stone, Beirne Spragins, Rev. Harry Wade,

Judge Elbert Parsons, Jimmy Walker, Dr. Harvey Nelson, Milton Cummings, John Garrison, Gene Monroe, and Jack Langhorne.

The second half of the twentieth century started on a very bright note indeed for Huntsville. Within a matter of a few months, the University Center was opened and the Fort Bliss rocket team was relocated to Huntsville. According to *The Huntsville Times,* the Chamber of Commerce staff "took over as father confessor, guides and first-class assistants" in welcoming the incoming group.[28]

The University Center Gets Underway

The University of Alabama Center in Huntsville began classes on January 6, 1950 with an enrollment of 137 students, slightly less than the 200 the University had set as the minimum. At the time of its inception, the Center was not envisioned as a technical or engineering school, but rather was intended to "provide as many resources of the mother campus as possible to the people of North Alabama who were unable to attend classes in Tuscaloosa. The Center's goals were to provide basic college credit courses qualifying students for advanced standing, immediate employment, and general education and to also provide special informal adult educational activities."[29]

Dr. Morton acted as the Center's first Director. He had constituted the Chamber's 1948 ad hoc group as an official Huntsville Center Advisory Committee. According to Patrick Richardson, the makeup of that Advisory Committee became the nucleus of the University of Alabama Huntsville Foundation Board of Trustees.

This group was composed of Lernon Pinkston, the Secretary of the Huntsville-Madison County Chamber of Commerce; Ed Burwell, the Director of the Veterans' Training Program of the Madison County Board of Education; Woodrow Dunn, Manager of Huntsville Manufacturing Company; Tom G. Thrasher, oil-dealer and President of the Huntsville Board of Education; and Vance J. Thornton, Realtor and President of the Huntsville City Council.

Students took classes in 10 sections of seven basic freshman subjects including accounting, economics, English, history, mathematics, political science and speech. Classes were held from 6 to 10 p.m. in the West Huntsville High School building[30] (the building was later named S.R. Butler High School and today is known as Stone Middle School). Registration cost $2, plus $4 for each credit hour.[31]

The initial faculty included Richardson, who taught economics; Walter Mills, chief fiscal officer at Rohm and Haas (a local defense contractor); Mamie Steger, chairman of the math department at West Huntsville; Mary Casmus, who was sent from Tuscaloosa to teach the first English classes, and Frances Roberts, then a social studies teacher at Huntsville High School.

Enrollment steadily climbed as did the region's population, and by the fall of 1953, three full-time faculty members and a part-time staff were teaching more than 250 students. Facilities became crowded and two former store buildings nearby were rented by the University for classes.[32]

In September 1951, the Redstone Arsenal Institute of Graduate Studies began offering graduate courses through UA's graduate school to military and civil service employees at Redstone. Supported by a federal contract (which ended in 1953), the graduate institute wasn't formally linked to the Huntsville Center, which furnished classroom space and scheduled the classes. The Huntsville Center did offer some graduate classes in non-technical areas.

By June of 1951, employment on the re-born Arsenal had swelled to over 5,000 and production on the once-idle munitions lines had resumed.[33]

The Rocket Programs Change the Community
The Germans were known to have referred to their time in the deserts of Fort Bliss as their "years of wandering in the wilderness,"[34] with little progress being made in the science and technology of missiles, propulsion, guidance and control. At their new home, they began making up for those idle days, and it wasn't

long before new technologies and new rocket systems were being developed.

Articles by von Braun and other space leaders in the popular *Collier's* magazine in 1952 and 1953 brought high-profile attention to both the rocket team and Huntsville.

The community was quick to capitalize on its new position in the spotlight of the fledgling world of guided missiles. Previous city marketing materials had dubbed Huntsville as the "Heart of the Tennessee Valley."[35] With the May 13, 1953 release of Chamber of Commerce sponsored pamphlets, "The Rocket City" became Huntsville's new nickname. The cover, "streamlined and colorful," depicted a rocket embarking for the moon from the earth. Its pages included Huntsville scenes of its industries, hospital, schools and other landmarks, plus brief descriptions and statistical data.

Chamber Secretary Jimmy Walker reported that 35,000 folders were ordered. Soon the word "rocket" was plastered everywhere in the city and included businesses such as the Rocket City Café and Rocket City Upholstery, among others.

On August 20, 1953, the Huntsville rocket team successfully launched its first Redstone missile from Cape Canaveral. Von Braun and his team soon quietly proposed the launch of a small orbital satellite, but concerns about international "saber rattling" kept the U.S. Army team from being the first to conquer space.

In spite of its "Rocket City, USA" moniker, the change in community mindset from so-called sleepy southern city to high-tech powerhouse did not occur overnight. A film prepared by the Chamber of Commerce for the city's 1955 sesquicentennial celebration harked back almost entirely to Huntsville's antebellum history of hoop-skirts. The community's space-faring exploits that lay just on the horizon were scarcely mentioned.

In 1955, the HIEC celebrated its first decade with prominent farmer-businessman Carl T. Jones serving as its president. By then the HIEC had been successful in locating more industry to the region, including the P.R. Mallory Company and Norton Company.

A new model for economic development was evolving that included traditional industrial recruitment coupled with readily available industrial sites outfitted with the necessary infrastructure. At the time, however, Huntsville had no publicly owned "green field" industrial parks in the city.

As is often the case, highway development would give rise to economic development opportunities. Growth would be directed away from the traditional center of commerce in the downtown region, to the west and south of the city, along the new Memorial

Parkway (named in memory of all fallen U.S. veterans) beginning in 1955.

In 1956, when plans for Alabama Highway 20 to the west of Huntsville were approved, the proposed right-of-way cut across the northwest corner of the Arsenal. Representatives from the HIEC persuaded the Army to declare the property north of the proposed highway to be surplus to the needs of the Arsenal.[36] "A group of 30 community leaders," realizing the importance of having land available for industrial purposes, formed a corporation to bid for the property when it was put up for auction in Atlanta.[37] The original investors included Carl T. Jones, M. B. Spragins*, C. S. Boswell, Robert K. Bell*, Charles Crute Thomas*, S. Gibson, George Mahoney*, William H. Stevens, Vance J. Thornton*, W. L. "Will" Halsey, Jr. *, Patrick Richardson, and Kenneth Noojin (* also served as President/Chairman of the Huntsville Chamber of Commerce).

About $70,000 was raised at $500 per share of stock (most of it with borrowed money) and a successful bid of $52,576.01 was made for the 248-acre tract.

According to Louis Salmon, most of those who contributed to the corporation thought it was a non-profit corporation, but it was incorporated as Huntsville Industrial Sites, Inc. a business corporation. HIS would later become Research Sites Foundation

(RSF) and ultimately it would change its name to the University of Alabama Huntsville Foundation.

The first sale of land by Huntsville Industrial Sites was to Ideal Baking Company (Sunbeam Bread), a tract of 2.37 acres for a total price of $7,500 or about $3,100 an acre. Considering the original purchase price of $212 an acre, this was nicely profitable.[38] Using a portion of those proceeds, HIS purchased a 116-acre tract of land on the Memorial Parkway South. With these transactions, HIS would establish the modus operandi for the economic development efforts of the community for years to come: Buy land at a good price, use it to attract industry, and book at least a modest profit so that more land could be acquired, market prices controlled and speculation averted for future development. During its early years, the presidents of HIS were County Attorney Robert K. "Buster" Bell, Kenneth Noojin, and Vance Thornton.

While there are no official records of the HIEC from the 1940s through the 1950s, at some point in the 1950s the HIEC hired its first paid staffer. According to Guy Nerren, who would become the second director of the HIEC in 1960, Jack Elliott, who had previously been the manager of Huntsville Manufacturing, was the first paid HIEC staffer. "Jack Elliott was highly respected in the community and did part-time work for the HIEC and he was the first full-time executive director," Nerren said.[39]

In 1955, the city's population stood at 50,000, it had three national banks with deposits of $32,000,000, and 40 industries employing 7,000. The Arsenal's employment at that time was 7,500 with a payroll of $2 million/month. Farm income for Huntsville/Madison County stood at $30 million and included seven nurseries. Transportation systems included two airlines; two railroads, three bus lines, and 10 truck lines. The community was also served by three radio stations.[40]

The final step in the Americanization of the German rocket team came on April 15, 1955, a red-letter day for Huntsville, when a group of 103 members of the von Braun team and their families became U.S. citizens in a mass naturalization ceremony organized by the Rotary Club.[41] The ceremony was held in the auditorium of Huntsville High School and an estimated 1,200 citizens turned out for the event. Von Braun told locals that it was "one of the proudest and most significant days of my life...almost like getting married. I am very, very happy."[42]

General Toftoy recalled during the ceremony: "I met you 10 years ago almost to the day in a crowded schoolhouse in Germany. I urged you to come to this country and help in our missile program. I promised you no future..." He concluded by congratulating them now that their highest hopes had been realized.

By the end of the decade, the City's population would soar to over 70,000, an incredible increase of over 56,000 people and a rate of over 340 percent in the 10-year period from 1950.[43]

In many respects, these were the early salad days for Huntsville. Employment on the Arsenal and in the defense/aerospace sector was booming and the demand for office space was keen. Even old textile mills found new life as office space for high-tech companies.

In 1957, when the huge Lincoln Mill textile manufacturing plant closed, Carl Jones and several HIEC members formed Huntsville Industrial Associates, Inc. and purchased the property in hopes of attracting other industry to the area. Although regarded by some as a risky investment, the old mill complex was soon transformed into the Huntsville Industrial Center. At its peak, the HIC structure would house 6,000 aerospace employees with a payroll in excess of $30 million.[44]

But industry wasn't the only thing quickly outgrowing existing facilities. Within four years of the University Center's founding, *Huntsville Times* editor and Huntsville Center Advisory Council member Reese Amis wrote that "...we may look forward to the time when it [the University Center] will have its own building and equipment..."[45] That time would come sooner rather than later.

In 1958, the Huntsville City Council purchased an 82-acre tract of land west of the city and north of the Arsenal situated between University Drive and Holmes Avenue. At the time this acreage, the Swartz farm, was purchased, no specific, announced development plan existed, although the University may well have been on at least some leaders' minds. *The Huntsville Times* editorialized against the purchase.

The Huntsville City Schools board had set aside 12 acres next to what is today Huntsville High School for the University at school board member Tom Thrasher's suggestion. But not long after the purchase of the Swartz property, Reese Amis and a group of other community leaders approached the City Council about using the property for the fast-growing University Center. "I think that by that time Mr. Amis was envisioning a full-blown university here, and I had begun to have dreams along that line," Pat Richardson stated in a 2001 interview.[46] City Council President Vance Thornton was persuaded to offer the City's property for the University Center.

The University Center was teaching several graduate courses in engineering, mathematics, and physics. Undergraduate classes included art, English, history, biology, chemistry, physics, economics, political science, Russian, German, French, accounting, marketing, management, business law, engineering, psychology, and sociology. Up to three years towards a baccalaureate degree could be completed in Huntsville; the remaining year was required to be taken in residence at the University of Alabama in Tuscaloosa.[47]

From the time the first students registered for classes at the University Center, the demographics of the student body were unusual. Initially the average age of the students was 30 and 95 percent of them were men, most of whom were veterans. In its early days, the University Center did not draw the numbers of recent local and area high school graduates that its supporters had anticipated.

In August of 1958, cotton broker-turned-aerospace industrialist Milton K. Cummings and banker Beirne Spragins, Sr. made a request of the Madison Board of County Commissioners to put up one-third of $750,000 to build a facility for the University Center. According to press reports of the meeting, a committee had been studying the possible locations and finance options for the facility[48].

That committee was composed of car dealer Louis Lee Sr., representing the City, lawyer Pat Richardson, of the city Board of Education, and James Record, county clerk-auditor, representing the County Commission. Record, perhaps not so coincidentally, was the first person awarded a certificate of proficiency in accountancy by the University Center in 1953.

The committee recommended that the City of Huntsville, Madison County and the University of Alabama each put up $15,000 annually for 30 years to finance the $750,000 building. It's worth noting that the part-time county attorney was Robert K. Bell, one of the leaders of the university effort. With perhaps more than a tinge of civic pride, Pat Richardson would later note that the University of Alabama did not actually need to come up with any money for this first building, since student fees repaid the loan the University secured for its portion of the building costs.

Clearly, Huntsville's leadership was not waiting for someone else to solve its problems. By George, if Huntsville needed a university, then the city and county fathers would take the initiative in developing one.

Another Huntsville tradition was also well established by this time. The assignment of roles and missions among and within the military services involve a constant give and take, a steady push and pull. Redstone would win more than its share of these battles, but it would lose some important ones from time to time.

The community and the Army lost several important inter-service battles in the early stages of the space race with the Soviet Union. Rivalries would confound but not derail Redstone's missile development work though. A serious struggle evolved over the important task of developing long-range missiles – and U.S. space projects. On July 29, 1955, President Dwight D. Eisenhower endorsed a Naval Research Laboratory space satellite proposal called "Project Vanguard." The von Braun team, although disappointed, continued its work on the 200-mile Redstone rocket and longer-range Jupiter missile.

On September 20, 1956, the first Jupiter C (modified Redstone rocket) attained a record-setting range of 3,300 miles, an altitude of 600 miles and a speed of 16,000 mph. A Presidential directive had prohibited the ignition of the fourth stage of the rocket, which would have placed the first object in space and given the United States the upper hand in the infant space race with the Soviet Union. Less than two months later the Army team would be "rewarded" when Secretary of Defense Charles E. Wilson ordered that the mission for longer-range missiles (beyond a 200-mile range) would go to the Air Force. Even as it lost the mission responsibility for work on the Jupiter intermediate range ballistic missile (IRBM), its work continued on the program.

The launch of Sputnik 1 on October 4, 1957 by the Russians would thrust Huntsville to the forefront of the U.S. side of the space race. Perhaps it was serendipity that the new Secretary of Defense-designate, Neil McElroy, was enjoying cocktails that evening at the Redstone Arsenal Officers Club with other visiting Washington officials, local military brass and community leaders. Dr. von Braun seized the opportunity to pitch his modified Redstone rocket, the Jupiter C, as the launch vehicle to answer the Soviet volley. Recalling the evening's activities many years later, Will Halsey would say that "there were so many general officers there that evening, the three-star generals were serving cocktails to the four-star generals."

Speaking to Secretary McElroy, von Braun said, "Sir, when you get back to Washington you'll find that all hell has broken loose. I wish you would keep one thought in mind through all the noise and confusion: we can fire a satellite into orbit 60 days from the moment you give us the green light."[49] Army Secretary Wilber Brucker, also attending the dinner that evening, expressed concern over the extremely short timeline. Redstone Commander John Bruce Medaris moderated the Redstone/Army launch commitment to 90 days from the date they received the green light. After initially winning the bid to put the first U.S. payload into earth orbit, the Navy soon failed with its Vanguard missile, and von Braun and company were at the ready.

On January 31, 1958 at 10:48 PM, the Redstone team launched the Jupiter-C Rocket RS-29 with the Explorer 1, the first U.S. satellite, circling the globe. A special "Satellite EXTRA" edition of *The Huntsville Times* dated February 1, 1958 detailed the city celebrations that accompanied the good news. Banner headlines declared "Jupiter-C Puts Up Moon – Wail of Sirens Brings In Era on Space Here." Sub-heading text exclaimed the jubilant celebration that ensued; "Thousands Gather On The Square For Noisy Success Demonstration" and announcing that "The wail of sirens, blasting horns and the fiery trails of store-bought rockets ushered in the country's first step toward the conquest of space at Huntsville last night."

With a not-so-subtle reference to frustrations born of the foregone opportunities denied to the von Braun team to be the first in the race to enter space, the story *in bold type* said, "As thousands of people gathered on the Courthouse Square, the one generally held responsible for much of the Army's troubles – former Secretary of Defense Charles E. Wilson – was burned in effigy, while thousands cheered..."

The accomplishment drew national attention to Huntsville as "representatives of *Life* magazine mingled with crowds along with newsmen from area newspapers" during the spontaneous downtown celebration.

But a cautious President Eisenhower fretted over having the military in the space business. On October 1, 1958 the President created a new civilian agency, the National Aeronautics and Space Administration (NASA), with jurisdiction over the U.S. space activities.

About a year later, on October 21, 1959, Eisenhower approved the transfer of more than 4,000 of Army Ballistic Missile Agency's scientists and engineers at Redstone to NASA. Six days later, the

Army Chief of Ordnance advised the Army Ordnance Missile Center that the Army's work for the civilian space agency would be handled under the Cooperative Agreement of December 3, 1958. ABMA's Development Operations Division, with von Braun as its technical director, would remain an Army responsibility until phased to NASA after Congressional approval. The transferees would remain at Redstone at a new NASA Field Center to be created in mid-1960.

Just as the previous decade had heralded new local demands for higher education, the 1950s would end with a plea for even greater support. On June 23, 1959, Major General Medaris, the Commander at the Arsenal, told the Alabama Legislature that if the state wanted to benefit from technology-oriented industrial growth, "a fundamental requirement is the creation of graduate study facilities and research centers to provide and sustain scientists and engineers. It seems to me highly important that the University in Huntsville be expanded to a full-scale, four-year college at the earliest practicable date."[50]

The decade of the 1950s was full of incredible growth, achievement, and challenge for Huntsville and Madison County. Who, at that time at the end of the 1950s, could have imagined that the growth, achievement, and challenge ahead would eclipse everything they had experienced?

Chapter Four: The Boom Of The Early `60s

Huntsville's Research Park and Research Institute Fuel Area's Growth

Just as the previous decade had begun with the establishment of several vital new local enterprises – chief among them the University Center and the new missile mission for Redstone Arsenal – the decade of the 1960s kicked off with enormous strides for the community and surrounding area.

On July 1, 1960, more than 4,000 U.S. Army personnel, including Dr. Wernher von Braun and his old German V2 team, along with about 1,900 acres of Redstone Arsenal, were transferred to the nation's new civilian space agency, NASA. Included were extensive rocket R&D and test facilities. Two months later, on September 8, 1960, President Eisenhower personally dedicated the fledgling field center, named in memory of his old friend and comrade-in-arms, the late General George C. Marshall.

Those changes on the Arsenal had kindled a certain anxiety in the local business community about the future of Huntsville's critical federal programs. "Congress had created NASA, von Braun had been pulled out of the Army and those were some [uncertain] days as far as where Huntsville was going to go and where the space program was going to go," according to Guy Nerren, who back then had recently become the top professional leading the community's economic development team.

Early in 1960, the Huntsville Industrial Expansion Committee had contracted with Fantus Area Research, Inc. to do a study of Huntsville and Madison County. The objective: to assess the area's prospects for industrial expansion and to outline a program of action. One of the first recommendations of the study was to establish a full-time economic development office staffed with experienced personnel.[51] Nerren was hired as the first full-time executive director of the HIEC in 1960 and was the first "professional" economic development expert to work in the community. He would soon become the widely acknowledged dean of such industrial recruiters in the state.

Nerren had worked the preceding four years for the Mississippi Delta Council, a regional economic and community development organization. "The Council had started in the early '20s as a volunteer-based, flood-control organization that grew into cotton, rice and soybean promotion. When the farmers realized they were not going to be able to pay the taxes for the land, they wanted industry to come in to employ the people," Nerren said in a 2006 interview.

"They [Fantus] did a study for Huntsville and previously had done a study for us in Mississippi, and that's the way my name got to

Huntsville. The truth of the matter is, all my peers who had been approached about the job [with the Huntsville Industrial Expansion Committee] had turned it down because it [Huntsville] was thought of as too much of a 'government town' and you could never attract industry to a town like that," added Nerren. "But of course they were wrong, [and] that was just the luck of the draw."

At the time, the field of industrial development was relatively new. According to Nerren: "Nobody went to school to study economic geography and economic development. Nowadays, people go to school to study computers and program things with economic models."

Huntsville industrialist Harry Moore Rhett, Jr. was chairman of the HIEC, Will Halsey was vice-chairman, and Tom Thrasher and Louis Salmon also were officers. "The people who were really in charge of Huntsville were Robert K. 'Buster' Bell, Carl T. Jones and [banker] Mr. Beirne Spragins," Nerren recalled. "If they decided to do something, you better watch out [because] it was going to happen. If they decided it was the wrong thing to do, it was *not* going to happen. I learned very quickly that if they didn't like the way that I parted my hair, I'd be gone. The HIEC Executive Committee included Alvin Blackwell, William "Bill" Stevens and a few others."

The budget for the HIEC was relatively modest in 1960. "When I was the executive director…we had a budget of $25,000. I made $12,000 and the part-time secretary and I were housed (rent free) at the Chamber," remembered Nerren.

While the HIEC had placed its initial emphasis in the mid- and late 1940s on diversifying Huntsville's economy away from defense-related industry, that sector became another important target for the HIEC recruiting efforts as the defense and space business boomed in the 1950s and `60s. The first project that Nerren recalled working on was Parker Aircraft Company, which leased space in the Huntsville Industrial Center.

In 1961 Brown Engineering became the first company to announce plans to leave the old Huntsville Industrial Center (HIC) complex for greener pastures near the under-construction and as-yet-unnamed University Center building.

Brown had been a struggling tool-and-dye and engineering operation when cotton magnate Milton Cummings and five local businessmen bought the company with $50,000, all borrowed locally, in the mid-1950s. Brown Engineering, originally Marietta Tool & Die, had relocated to Huntsville from Georgia in July 1953. Over the years with Cummings' involvement as president of the company, his excellent political connections and business acumen quickly helped turn the company around. Brown's local annual payroll doubled every year for the next four years – from $55,000 in 1955 to $4,529,000 in 1959.[52]

At first Brown operated in a building on the southwest corner of Governors Drive and Memorial Parkway. It soon moved to the HIC building, joining a number of other aerospace employers. But in 1960, Brown executive Joseph Moquin and co-owner Milton Cummings decided to move Brown's operations to the area near the new University facilities.

The site lay on Sparkman Road, an unpaved farm road at that time, connecting Governors Drive and University Drive. Brown's executive vice president (and later president), Joe Moquin, later recalled he had been approached by a Marshall Space Flight Center representative with an urgent request to lease additional office space.

"He asked me if we could rent him any space; I had gone through a lot of background about the HIC building and then I told him, 'I know where you can rent space, not immediately, but very shortly.' And we arrived at a verbal agreement. I went to Milton and the board, and I told them, 'Now, as far as I'm concerned, if you don't support me on this, you're probably not going to have me because I want out of this location.' I said we should do the right thing, and it would have to be done rapidly in order to make some kind of formal agreement with Marshall."

For Moquin, the right thing was to build a pre-fabricated manufacturing facility in short order, then move Brown Engineering's professional and overhead people into it. "Well, I got quite a reaction from the Board of Directors who said you can't move professional people into a pre-manufactured building."

Moquin had been gathering ammunition for this fight for the last two years. "I had already identified the proper place for this on what is now known as Sparkman Road. I was quite familiar with the fact that most of the land was very open, some of it pasture land, a good bit of it had trees on it, and I thought it was the right kind of land to be developed. And I considered two very important factors. One was its accessibility to Marshall Space Flight Center and to the [Army] Missile Command [at Redstone]. But there was another factor I considered very important. It was close to the one building the University of Alabama in Huntsville had. For a company in our kind of advanced technology work, being close to a university would be an important factor." He also noted "it was in a relatively large area that could be properly zoned." Finally, Brown's board agreed.

With that approval, Moquin asked Cummings about buying 360 acres. While he didn't really need all that acreage, Moquin said it would enable better infrastructure and promote partnerships with other companies. It wasn't long before Brown had sold property to IBM and Northrop.

Two people were key to efforts in establishing the larger Research Park, said Moquin: Charles Cummings, Jr., a member of the City Council and the nephew of Milton Cummings, and Dean Y. Mathews, the head of Huntsville city planning. Moquin talked to them about the relatively large area that could be properly zoned. "On one side of the highway [then Rideout Road, now Research Park Boulevard], it had limited access; there was about 1,000 acres. On the other side, there was about another 2,000 acres [reaching] to the city limits. I told Charles I supported at least 1000 acres in the initial park, and that I'd like the City Council and the city planner to initiate the proper steps." Moquin even supplied what he thought should be some basic conditions. "A company that went out there should primarily be a high-technology company and not a major manufacturer," he reasoned. "Manufacturing should be support to the major engineering, design and analysis capability, but should not be primary or have a significant amount of manufacturing."

According to Moquin, one of the first things Mathews did was go to Research Triangle Park in North Carolina. "When he came back, he recommended going from a thousand to 3,000 acres. It was amazing just how quickly the City Council responded by zoning that entire area as a Research Park." Giving further credit, Moquin observed that Charlie Younger in the city attorney's office did the massive amount of work toward the Research Park zoning, which was completed in 1962. [53]

Brown's payroll would more than double from $4,100,000 in 1960 to $10,000,000 in 1962 when it occupied over 240,000 square feet of office space in the Research Park.[54]

Another Huntsville start-up was likewise enjoying great success at this same time. Space Craft, Inc., later known as SCI Systems, grew rapidly from its inauguration in July 1961 with seven employees to over 250 employees in 40,000 square feet of office space by late 1963.

Enrollment at the University Center was also growing quickly by this time, climbing to more than 1,100 in 1960.

The space race with the Soviet Union was front and center in the 1960 presidential campaign and in the public's consciousness. On April 12, 1961, just a few months after President John F. Kennedy's inauguration, the Soviets scored another space "first" when cosmonaut Yuri Gagarin became the first human to enter space and orbit Earth. America grew anxious over the strong Soviet lead in the race to conquer space.

Eighteen days after Gagarin's flight, on May 1, 1961, astronaut Alan B. Shepard, a U.S. Navy officer, became the first American to enter space. His chariot, a modified Redstone "Jupiter C" rocket, boosting a one-seat Mercury capsule, came compliments of Huntsville's Marshall Space Flight Center and the U.S. Army at Redstone.

Emboldened by Shepard's 17-minute suborbital ride, President Kennedy would soon challenge the Congress and the nation to set an ambitious objective in the cosmic race that he believed the U.S. could achieve first. On May 21, 1961, just three weeks after Shepard's brief excursion, Kennedy, in an address to a joint session of the Congress, called for the nation to land a man on the moon and return him safely to earth by the end of the decade, giving birth to Project Apollo.

Work on development and clustering of the powerful Saturn V engines that would be needed to boost men and equipment to the moon had begun in 1958 and had been authorized by the Defense Department's Advanced Research Projects Agency (ARPA), since the Army had no mission for such a vehicle.[55] In November, 1958, ARPA gave the go-ahead to build four flight test vehicles and to develop multi-stage Saturn launch vehicles. Following President Kennedy's challenge, work on the new systems began at a feverish pitch.

According to then-HIEC Vice-Chairman Will Halsey, the community realized the timing was right to have von Braun speak to the Alabama Legislature: "We decided to ask if the state Legislature would let a number of businesspeople from Huntsville escort Wernher von Braun to the state Legislature to address them. We finally got that permission, and we took two military aircraft from the Arsenal. We took about 40 people down there to hear von Braun address the [lawmakers]."[56] One month after the President laid the lunar challenge at the Congress' feet, Dr. von Braun, on June 21, 1961, addressed a joint session of the Alabama Legislature with a challenge of his own.

Von Braun's vision for his adopted home of Huntsville included a strong research and development environment bolstered by a research park where industry could locate. It also embraced a research institute, where his employees could obtain advanced technical degrees and pioneer new technologies for future generations of space vehicles. On this June day, he would sell the Legislature on the need for additional funding to support a research institute at the new University Center in Huntsville.

The initiative for a research institute began "when a group from Redstone Arsenal recommended to the president of the university on June 13, 1960, that educational programs be expanded in Huntsville and that a research institute be established,"[57] according to Pat Richardson. It was established on October 1 of that year on an interim basis with personnel loaned by main-campus departments.[58] University of Alabama President Frank Rose agreed, and on January 24, 1961, MSFC funded the first work done by the Research Institute.[59] The institute, however, lacked facilities and was operating in office space owned by Brown Engineering.[60]

Among von Braun's many considerable skills were his phenomenal communication abilities. Those powers were never in greater evidence than in his June 1961 address to a joint session of Legislature. He established instant rapport with his audience by greeting them first by saying that "it is a very real honor for me, a citizen of Alabama, to address you today in the Capital City of our Great State." Next he thanked Governor John M. Patterson and the Legislature for their help. Compliments, honest and sincere, came for the state government's role in welcoming and supporting the rocket and space work done in Alabama.

Then the rocket engineer-scientist told the simple story of Benjamin Franklin and his kite and the vast, unforeseeable benefits born of human curiosity – and scientific enterprise. "Curiosity gave us penicillin," he noted. He quoted Henry Ward Beecher saying that "the soul without imagination is what an observatory would be without a telescope."

The question on everyone's mind, of course, was how far was America behind the Soviets in the space race and how were we going to get to the moon?

Von Braun showed the lawmakers slides of the Redstone "family" of rockets that had placed the Explorers I, III, and IV satellites into space and taken Alan Shepard on his arching, sub-orbital ride. Next came a detailed briefing on the rockets that would take the United

States to the moon, including a view-graph that showed a scaled-model comparison of the Saturn V on the grounds of the Alabama State Capitol. Von Braun spoke of future nuclear rockets and missions to Mars, and space stations and such, but with a steady, matter-of-fact confidence. And then he began his beautifully crafted sales pitch for the research institute.

First, he threw some large numbers at the legislators, including the number of employees working at Redstone, Marshall's payroll, and the combined NASA and Army spending in Alabama. Then, ever so delicately, he brought up the educational requirements of the new high-tech workforce:

> "This, I submit," said von Braun, "is substantial evidence to show that opportunity is indeed knocking on Alabama's door, and knocking hard, just as opportunity knocked on California's door a few decades ago when the aircraft industry was beginning to blossom. The question is, 'will Alabama open the door?'

> "As a proud citizen of this state and of this country, I feel a responsibility to raise this question with you and to discuss it openly and frankly.

Von Braun quoted Shakespeare, 'There is a tide in the affairs of man, which, taken at its flood, leads on to fortune.' For Alabama, the tide is at flood now – but is passing fast. My appeal to you is to recognize this and to take action today while the opportunity is still available. I am sure there are very few problems in Alabama which could not be solved with more money – the proper capital investment at this time can produce that money for the State of Alabama."

"To make Huntsville more attractive to technical and scientific people – and to further develop the people we have now – the academic and research environment of Huntsville and Alabama must be improved immediately."

Von Braun pitched the University Center, Research Institute and the concept of an industrial research park as a part of the University complex, "which in turn will give birth to major new industries throughout the state." He rhetorically asked what brought the aviation industry to Los Angeles - "The desert and smog? No, it was U.C.L.A and Cal Tech and the Art Institute and St. Mary's and the University of Southern California." He continued:

"Was it beans that brought great electronic and other industries to Boston? It was the Educational Triangle of Boston University, Harvard and M.I.T.

"Let's be honest with ourselves about it: it's not water or real estate, or labor, or power, or cheap taxes that brings industry to a state or city. It's *brainpower,*" von Braun emphasized. "Nowadays, brainpower dumped in a desert will make it rich. Right now you could run a profitable electronics firm on the moon, if the company liked the climate. Educational climate, that is."[61]

The response from the Legislature was dramatic and immediate. "They were overcome with the opportunity," according to Will Halsey.[62] In a body where consensus can be hard to achieve, the two chambers of the Legislature unanimously voted to approve the proposal to invest $3 million in the Research Institute in Huntsville.

The State's funding commitment required a public referendum on the bond issue to underwrite the funding. "Well, that threw some problems in," recalled Halsey. "The members of the HIEC knew a number of people from across the state, and they did a lot of telephoning and the thing was voted on statewide. And I think it passed by about three to one." The bond issue was approved by the voters of Alabama on December 5, 1961.

Huntsville and Madison County then agreed to provide $400,000 to the University for the purchase of an additional 200 acres on which to construct the new Institute, although the Research Institute and University Center were not organizationally connected.[63]

Construction of UAH's first building – a combination administrative and classroom facility – had been completed in December of 1960 and opened for classes the following month. The building was named for John R. Morton, the Extension Center Division director and first administrator of the University Center. It was dedicated on May 6, 1961, as Morton Hall.

With Brown Engineering, the Research Institute, and the University Center all located along Sparkman Road, the area was primed for future development.

The Research Park zoning ordinance created by the City in 1962 specified the types of suitable business activity permissible within the 3,000-acre park borders. It restricted businesses to R&D and high-technology manufacturing. Speculative building was expressly prohibited, a restriction that would be tested by more than one company.

"Brown was going to develop an industrial park themselves," Guy Nerren recalled. "There is nothing wrong with that, that is a normal business enterprise. But the foundation [Huntsville Industrial Sites] came along and cut their legs out from under them, as it should have done, because this was a community project."

Accounting executive David Johnston later recalled: "When Brown bought that land in the area that would become the Research Park and started developing those buildings I think that was a wake-up call for the development community, all property owners and the other leaders of the city."[64]

However, von Braun had become concerned about land speculation and potential profiteering in the Research Park, or in any industrial property held by groups of community leaders. Some of those involved in the early stages of the development of the Research Park have also speculated – off the record – that von Braun may have been encouraged to halt Cummings's development of the Research Park by others with similar interests in the community.

Von Braun called the board members of the Huntsville Industrial Sites and the HIEC out to meet with him. "The first sale of Research Park property was thought to be too high to attract prospects, so Huntsville Industrial Sites decided to acquire land within the Research Park zoning area," lawyer Louis Salmon said.[65]

Von Braun had said, although he knew Huntsville Industrial Sites (and Brown) were not trying to make unreasonable profits from land sales, they nevertheless were a profit-oriented business corporation.

He, in his position as director of Marshall Space Flight Center, could not allow his name to be associated with the park or any such for-profit enterprise. Von Braun "talked to the leadership of the Huntsville Industrial Expansion Committee, explaining that he couldn't very well twist the arms of his contractors to come to Huntsville just to put money in the pockets of land speculators," Pat Richardson would recall.[66]

"His direct comment, in his unique accent was, 'I can just see what [syndicated muckraking columnist] Drew Pearson will have to say about me and my involvement with the Park.'" [67]

Guy Nerren recalled that "they let me tag along" to the meeting. "Von Braun said, 'Gentlemen, I want to do everything I can to promote Huntsville, and to get industry here.' But – holding up a Birmingham newspaper - I can't remember exactly what it said, but the politicians there had been caught in some sort of land deal where they were making money [improperly], he said, 'I can't have this happen to me. You have to create an entity here that will be nonprofit if you want my participation in recruiting industry here.'"[68] Asked what to do, von Braun advised: Form a foundation.

As von Braun suggested, Research Sites Foundation was organized as a 501 (c)(6) not-for-profit land-holding arm of the Huntsville Industrial Expansion Committee, on October 24, 1962. As a 501 (c)(6) (so-named for the section of the Internal Revenue Code that defined such entities), the corporation was non-profit, paid no income taxes, but neither were contributions to it tax-deductible. The initial board of directors for Research Sites Foundation consisted of: Robert K. Bell, Daniel C. Boone, W.L. Halsey, Jr., Carl T. Jones, O. Howard Moore, F.K. Noojin, Harry M. Rhett, Jr.; Patrick W. Richardson, Charles E. Shaver, M. B Spragins, Vance J. Thornton, and Thomas G. Thrasher. The registered agent was lawyer Jerry B. Tucker, and Guy Nerren was the secretary. According to the bylaws, "The sole purpose of the corporation shall be to serve in any and all possible ways the interest of the University of Alabama Research Institute at Huntsville, Alabama."[69] The address listed was 200-208 Terry-Hutchens Building – the same address as the HIEC and the Chamber of Commerce.

The first meeting minutes kept today by the UAH Foundation date to January of 1962 and are from Huntsville Industrial Sites (HIS), whose founders were nearly identical to the list of Research Sites Foundation originators.

While the goal in structuring the new foundation was to make it a charitable organization, according to HIEC accountant David Johnston, those initial efforts to have the foundation qualified as a charitable 501(c)(3) had failed, but that battle had only just begun.

Research Sites Foundation initially purchased a 128-acre tract of land in the Research Park near the Research Institute. "The Research

Sites Foundation then bought 300 acres west of Sparkman Drive, east of Wynn Drive, north of Southern Railway and south of University Drive from Annie Bradford and resold it at a profit to research and development industries serving Marshall Space Flight Center and Redstone Arsenal," related Pat Richardson.[70]

At the time of its founding, HIS and the Research Sites Foundation were the only "public controlled organizations with land available for industry."[71]

Growth in and around Huntsville came at a blistering pace. By the end of 1962, the city of Huntsville and the Arsenal were about equal in size, at approximately 60 square miles. Employment on the Arsenal stood at about 30,000.[72]

Some years later, Mayor Joe Davis was approached by a local citizen, complaining about "traffic problems" and congestion on area roads. "I wouldn't call what we have today a 'traffic problem,'" Davis replied. "I can remember a time when you could lie down in the middle of Washington Street [in downtown Huntsville] in the middle of the day and not have to worry about being run over. *That is a traffic problem.*"

Chapter Five: The Birth Of The University of Alabama Huntsville Foundation

Growth for Huntsville, Madison County and the Marshall Space Flight Center came unabated through 1966. Construction at NASA's Marshall Center in 1964 alone would top $38 million and its budget would more than triple, going from under $400 million in 1962 to nearly $1.3 billion just two years later.

The effect on the Huntsville economy was breathtaking. In the first quarter of 1964 alone, retail sales achieved the second-fastest growth rate in the United States, to $61 million – up 19.3 percent over the same period in 1963.[73] Retail sales in the city for the full year rose from $184 million in 1963 to $218 million in 1964.

Non-Agricultural employment would soar from 46,270 in 1960 to more than 62,200 in 1963. Like many local aerospace contractors, Brown Engineering Company saw its employment rolls swell by 33 percent in just the last six months of 1963, rising from 3,000 on July 1, 1963 to 4,000 on December 31, 1963. Other aerospace industries were also expanding rapidly. At the other 30 aerospace businesses located in Huntsville, employment grew by 1,210 jobs during the same six-month period, with many companies doubling their personnel rolls.[74]

To accurately quantify the region's phenomenal growth, the City and County petitioned the federal government to perform a special census, which was taken September 22, 1964 through the U.S. Bureau of Census.

The only surprising finding of the mid-decade census was the extent to which the community had underestimated its stunning growth. Madison County's population increased a staggering 47.7 percent between 1960 and 1964, bringing the total number of residents to 173,285. Huntsville's population swelled by an even more extreme 70.7 percent in the four years from 1960 to 1964, from 72,365 to 123,519. Huntsville's geographical size also increased to 39 square miles through annexation during the same period.[75]

Even the rosiest, most optimistic growth projections proved too conservative. "Huntsville has pressed change to its bosom," Paul O'Neal reported in *Fortune* magazine in June of 1962. Huntsville bet huge sums of borrowed money to expand itself and provide for future development. Included: $7 million for a new water works; $4 million on a new gas system; $13 million on a new electric system; $10 million on new sewer systems. For seven straight years, from 1957 to 1963, the city averaged building one new school room a week.[76] The pace continued. Some 4,500 residential lots were approved for home development in 1964 alone.[77]

At the heart of much of this growth were the Research Sites Foundation and the Huntsville Industrial Expansion Committee (HIEC), which were managing the Research Park.

Minutes from the first year of the Research Sites Foundation's board meetings show brisk property sales in the Research Park. Buyers included Space Technology Laboratories, Tech Consolidated Inc., Thiokol, General Electric, Lear Siegler, Northrop and expressions of interest from AT&T, Aero-Jet General and Hayes Aircraft.

However, the Research Sites Foundation board faced a troubling prospect that could inhibit its effectiveness in economic development: It would face paying considerable taxes if it could not establish a charitable affiliation and thus shelter the proceeds from its property sales.

Originally the Research Sites Foundation, as the predecessor to the University of Alabama Huntsville Foundation, had no connections with the University or with higher education. "The Research Sites Foundation was a tool of economic development and really the University became the beneficiary of it because we had to have a nonprofit institution [as] beneficiary in order to receive the tax status," according to former HIEC director Guy Nerren. "Not to take away from the value of the University, but that was the bottom line"[78]

As Huntsville's economy boomed, it needed places to locate new industry. The HIEC was clearly the lead organization for economic expansion in the community, but it did not own property directly. By 1963, HIEC membership stood at 350 individuals and firms representing the business and professional leadership of the city.[79] The HIEC used Huntsville Industrial Sites and Research Sites Foundation to acquire property for industrial parks and business sites.

It was the perfect one-stop-shop for economic development – with somewhat blurred lines separating the various development-oriented organizations. The names and faces of the players remained essentially the same from one organization to the next.

The general thinking at the time of the Research Sites Foundation's creation was that the fruits of its real estate operations would somehow inure to the benefit of the Chamber or the Huntsville Industrial Expansion Committee. But ultimately that was not to be the case. It was, however, the good fortune of The University of Alabama in Huntsville and the many students, faculty and staff who have benefited that the following turn of events was to take place.

By 1963, von Braun's vision for a research park, owned and operated by a non-profit entity, was quickly taking shape. "The Huntsville Industrial Expansion Committee is engaged in a stepped-up program to seek new industries both related and unrelated to the missile and space industry, with their major emphasis concentrated on the Research Park project. Already 300 acres have been sold," the City stated in a 1964 report.[80]

While the goal at the time the Research Sites Foundation was constituted had been to make it a 501 (c)(3) (charitable) entity, the IRS would grant it only *non-profit*, 501 (c)(6) tax status, making contributions to it a business expense and not a charitable donation.

HIEC and Research Sites Foundation accountant David Johnston would later explain that "…the dilemma was finding areas [of operations and alliances] that would qualify for favorable tax treatment."

The tax rate in the early 1960s was high for big earners – as much as 50 to 70 percent – making income shelters especially attractive and making it imperative for this community development organization to become not just a non-profit entity, but a charitable organization. As a non-profit body with no charitable anchor, Research Sites Foundation had to be careful not to make too much money on real estate transactions, which were considered unrelated business income, or else it risked losing its non-profit status. That would force it to pay out a substantial portion of its equity in taxes.

"The dilemma was…the way that the Foundation was set up…the profit was subject to tax," David Johnston recalled.

Johnston explained that three basic recognized categories of not-for-profit organizations qualify for tax-deductible gifts: charitable, educational, or medical. As an organization dedicated to the development of the research park and otherwise for the economic expansion of the region, the Research Sites Foundation did not qualify for tax-deductible, charitable contributions, he pointed out.

Lawyer Louis Salmon and Johnston were named to a special committee of the for-profit Huntsville Industrial Sites in February of 1964 to study possible non-profit status for the corporation.[81] "The key thing for us was to try to mold what we really wanted to do within the tax code and get approval," remembered Johnston. When it became apparent that turning HIS into a not-for-profit entity was impractical, other options were developed.

"Our goal was to give the Huntsville Industrial Sites property to the Research Sites Foundation since it had…sold some land and it had equity; and it [also] had some land left, so we wanted to get that equity into Research Sites Foundation," Johnston said.

Deeply in debt but land rich, the Research Sites Foundation arranged to borrow $235,000 in March of 1964 to make scheduled payments for property, using the guaranty of Huntsville Industrial Sites as collateral.[82]

By August of that year, a plan had been developed to morph Research Sites Foundation into the University of Alabama Huntsville Foundation and request 501 (c)(3) status for the latter from the IRS. That plan was revealed at a September 8, 1964 meeting of the Research Sites Foundation board at the Russel Erskine Hotel. Patrick Richardson, president, chaired the meeting. Members attending included Vance Thornton, Dan Boone, Harry Rhett, Jr., Buster Bell, M.B. Spragins, Howard Moore, W.L. "Will" Halsey, Jr., Charles Shaver, Tom Thrasher and Guy Nerren. Also attending were Johnston, Salmon, and Clyde Reeves, the vice president for University Affairs at the University Center.

Salmon gave a detailed report of the meetings that his committee (appointed by Vance Thornton, president of HIS) had conducted and of the various organizational options investigated. Salmon's committee suggested a plan that called for Research Sites Foundation, Inc. to broaden its scope of activities to include granting scholarships, establishing chairs at the university, and otherwise furthering the development of the University Center and the Research Institute.

While 501(c)(3) tax status had not been granted, Salmon felt that the proposed changes to RSF would justify another application to the IRS for that preferred status. These proposed changes would enlarge the purposes of RSF and change the name of the corporation to the "University of Alabama Huntsville Foundation" and add the president of the University and the vice president of the University for Huntsville Affairs as members of the Board of Directors.

The motion to modify RSF's bylaws was approved unanimously. The board authorized the appointment of a special committee to go to Birmingham and to Washington, D.C., if necessary, at the expense of the corporation, to seek this approval. A delegation was also dispatched to meet with University officials.

"We then decided that since we're dealing with so many people and the reputation of the City and the Chamber and the HIEC, we ought to get an advance ruling that what we were doing would meet the IRS guidelines," David Johnston recalled. "Normally, what you would do is get your documents, file them and get a letter of approval and then you would begin your operations and the IRS would come see you later. But we wanted to get advance approval, and so we submitted the documents in advance."[83] Louis Salmon went to Washington to meet with the office of the Commissioner of Internal Revenue and was successful in obtaining a 501 (c) (3) status so that contributions to the Foundation would be tax-deductible.[84]

In December 1964, Salmon reported that the IRS's Birmingham revenue director had signaled his approval of the foundation as a tax-exempt entity provided it made certain modifications to its charter and by-laws. Those amendments were approved in October of 1965, at which time the name of the Research Sites Foundation was changed to the University of Alabama Huntsville Foundation. In recognition of his hard work to secure this important tax status, Salmon was added to the Foundation board on December 1 of that year.

Practically all of the shareholders of Huntsville Industrial Sites donated their stock to the University of Alabama Huntsville Foundation. The remaining shares were purchased by the University of Alabama Huntsville Foundation. "All but three shareholders made the contribution, and for each share contributed, the stockholders, who had paid $500 apiece for their shares originally, received an initial tax deduction of nearly $12,000. The rising fair-market value of the real property owned by Huntsville Industrial Sites had sharply increased the share value," according to Salmon.[85]

Several years would pass before the IRS would conclude its valuation assessment of the HIS assets donated to the UAH Foundation. The final value was set at $10,320.24 per share, according to David Johnston's report to the board on March 28, 1968.[86]

"The Research Sites Foundation, which had made most of its purchases with borrowed money from First National Bank [of Huntsville], thanks to [Board Chairman] Beirne Spragins, was now at last financially solvent," Salmon would later recall.[87]

A Research Park Advisory Board was organized in the latter half of 1964. It consisted of the representatives of companies located in the park and those who were building or in final negotiations to construct buildings in the park. One year later there were 13 members of the Advisory Board. "This group met monthly to study, analyze and recommend actions to make the Research Park the most desirable environment for the present industries to operate and to help promote continued growth and expansion," according to Advisory Board documents.[88] This organization interfaced directly with the HIEC, which managed the park.

An editorial in *The Huntsville Times* on August 29, 1965 beautifully summarized the astounding achievements of the HIEC and the Research Sites Foundation in the development of the Research Park:

> For more than a decade, the story of Huntsville has been a story of expansion. Statistics – the happy kind – have burgeoned until by now, only those with computer minds can carry half of them.

> Yet there was released on Friday, a set of figures capable of opening even Huntsvillians eyes wide. These had to do with expansion in the city's Research Park.

Acting as spokesman for the Huntsville Industrial Expansion Committee, Carl Jones informed the Madison County Board of Commissioners that 900,000 square feet of existing plant space now are in the Research Park area.

But that was only a starter in the HIEC report.

With 6,500 employed, the figure within the next 120 days will have reached 8,000. By July 1, it will exceed 10,000. By that same time, the payroll will greatly exceed $65 million a year.

In addition to 900,000 square feet now occupied, 300,000 more square feet is in the planning stage or under contract.

Three more industries – at least two of them, "blue chip" and big – are proposed to establish new facilities.

All this adds up to a story as amazing as any even today's Huntsville has to tell. Our Research Park has become one of the top areas of its kind in America.

It is a story which has a moral. "Research centers" had been laid out by cities and towns all across the nation. Many of them still remain in appearance if no longer in name cow pastures and uncultivated farmlands.

In short, it takes more than a sign over an entrance road to make a corn field a research center.

It takes long-range planning. It takes tireless dedication of the leadership of the community. It takes clearly defined and continuing evidence of a community willing to cooperate wholly and intelligently with prospective candidates for occupancy. It requires the catalyst of an atmosphere and locale conducive to continued growth.

These items Huntsville and the HIEC have applied without stint. The result has been fantastic success. And we believe Mr. Jones was not overstating the case when he remarked Friday that the future of Huntsville's Research Park "is so good it's almost unbelievable."

The HIEC report to the Madison County commissioners was coupled with a request for expedition of grading and paving work in the Research Park area necessary for construction of the new buildings now on the drawing boards. And there is no question, whatever, but that, once again, full cooperation for Madison County will be forthcoming.

As the editorial referenced, because the Research Park was being developed by a non-profit, university-affiliated organization, the State, City and County built roads and provided utilities without cost to the individual industries involved. This assistance further enabled the University of Alabama Huntsville Foundation to offer low per-acre cost to industries buying building sites. Under state law, city, county and state ad valorem taxes were routinely waived for new industry locating in the Park for a period of 10 years.[89]

Another incentive offered to new industries building in the Research Park was City-issued municipal revenue bonds for the construction of office space on a lease-back arrangement. These were tax-exempt bonds offering a considerable savings for industry.[90]

The Industrial Development Board (IDB) of the City of Huntsville was created by the City Council at its meeting on the 27th of May, 1965. City councilmen present were Thomas Dark, Ronald Pearsall, and Abner C. McNaron. Councilman John Rodenhauser was absent.

The City Council appointed the following to the industrial development Board: J. Edward Humphrey and George N. Robinson, two-year terms; Vance J. Thornton and W. L. Halsey, Jr., four-year terms; Tom Thrasher, Carl T. Jones and Charles Shaver, six-year terms. The IDB held its first meeting on June 3, 1965, at the Chamber of Commerce. Elected as officers were Thrasher, chairman; Halsey, vice-chairman; Guy B. Nerren, secretary, and Humphrey, treasurer.[91]

Through the HIEC and its affiliated organizations, Huntsville and Madison County's economic development team offered a comprehensive packaging of business development services – a "one-stop-shop" including marketing of its business and industrial parks, industrial property, site development (including utilities), tax abatements, and project financing.

The University Center Becomes A University
It was only natural for the University Center Advisory Committee, composed of those same industry leaders that were charting the business growth of the community, to want the University also to broaden and expand its operations. Growth of the Research Institute and the University Center's campus in its buildings and enrollment, pointed toward a future as an autonomous campus. The opportunity to formally air these opinions came in 1963.

Accreditation by the Southern Association of Colleges and Schools (SACS) required the University's Extension Division to submit a comprehensive report of its operations. In preparing the division's report, the University asked each of its extension centers to prepare a self-analysis of its operations. "This self-analysis concluded that the Huntsville Center should be given the status of a branch of the parent University," an historian noted.[92]

Responding to community pressures for greater autonomy, University of Alabama President Dr. Frank A. Rose named Dr. Charley Scott as director of instruction in Huntsville in June of 1963. In the fall of that year Dr. Clyde Reeves was appointed vice president for Huntsville Affairs.

Also in June of 1963, both the University and the community recognized that the Huntsville Center was on the "verge of becoming a full-service institution of higher learning" when University officials announced plans to award graduate degrees for work completed in Huntsville.[93]

Yet another important event took place that same month, when on June 13 – just two days after Gov. George C. Wallace's infamous "stand in the schoolhouse door" to attempt to keep black students from enrolling at the University of Alabama (in Tuscaloosa) – Huntsville's University Center enrolled its first black student. Without incident, African American David M. McGlathery, a mathematician at MSFC, enrolled in the center's graduate program.[94]

As progress of the young institution continued, in August of the next year Julian Palmore received his master's of science in mathematics, marking the first time a degree was awarded for work completed entirely on the Huntsville campus, although Palmore would have to travel to Tuscaloosa to receive his diploma.

Shortly after coming to the University, Clyde Reeves approached the University Advisory Committee about the need for additional facilities on the Huntsville campus. Once again community leaders Beirne Spragins and Will Halsey, Jr. would step forward to chair a fundraising campaign for the construction of Madison Hall. Huntsville businesses and citizens also stepped forward. "The goal was to raise $600,000, but they actually raised $900,000," Pat Richardson recalled many years later.[95]

"The University called me and said that we've got to have more money," Halsey recalled.[96] "They said that Wernher von Braun had talked to us and the University's comment was they wanted to know what the hell we were going to do. Wernher had said that we made one hell of a mistake – that we should have asked for $15 million to start with since it [the bond issue referendum for the original Research Institute] passed by three to one. But we couldn't get any more money out of the state at that time."

The extremely successful Madison Hall fundraising effort would involve donations from nearly 600 individuals, clubs, companies, and other organizations. Meticulously kept records by Will Halsey from that effort, dated January 15, 1965, show contributions ranging from a high of $30,000 (from Brown Engineering Company and Lockheed Corporation) to $5 each from several local citizens and small firms. Halsey's list contains the names of every individual and company that made contributions to the effort. It grouped those into several categories and gave the amounts raised from each:

Advance gifts (pledges)	$480,757.50
University alumni	5,680.00
Huntsville city school students	4,1256.86
Civic and professional clubs	4,243.00
Decatur	44,160.00
Dentists	7,915.00
Doctors	35,325.00
Faculty and staff	3,738.75
Guntersville	1,550.00
Employees of local companies	36,684.07
Lawyers	45,545.00
Local businesses	93,635.00
Missile industries	81,631.50
PTAs	1,541.56

The University Center would drop "Center" from its name in May of 1964 and become the Huntsville "Campus," and it would get its first direct state appropriation in 1965 of $800,000. Until then, the

University Center had functioned almost as a private school might, using only funds raised through registration fees and tuitions for its operations.

A regular day schedule of classes began in 1964. Enrollment at the University campus would jump to 2,042 by the fall of 1963, twice what it had been only a few years earlier.

Chapter Six: Growth Takes A Breather

"It's very simple: late to bed early to rise, work like hell, and advertise" –Wernher von Braun

The region's economic development machine would face its greatest challenges in the years following the phenomenal run-up in spending on Project Apollo in the space program. Saturn V launch vehicle development expenditures would peak in early 1966, fully three and a half years before the first successful manned moon-landing. Worker reductions were part of the downturn.   In 1965, aerospace and defense employment reached a high of 17,755; that figure would drop to 16,547 in 1966.[97]

In September of 1967, Dr. von Braun had worried aloud: "To make a one-night stand on the Moon and go there no more would be as senseless as building a railroad and then making only one trip from New York to Los Angeles."[98]   That, however, appeared to be the program's destiny.

In 1968, von Braun had this to say about the downsizing: "It may surprise you to hear this, but for the last two years, my main effort at the Marshall Center has been following orders to scrub the industrial structure that we had built up at great expense to the taxpayer, to tear it down again. The sole purpose seems to be to make sure that after

1972, nothing of our capability is left. That's my main job at the moment. And we haven't even put a man on the Moon yet."[99]

As von Braun predicted, more reductions would follow. However, the savvy group of local leaders that had helped to spearhead and facilitate the economic successes of the foregoing years had faced similar circumstances with Redstone Arsenal's decline in the post-WWII years. The economic "boom" of the space program was ending. Would there be a "bust" for the community?

It is noteworthy that none of the HIEC and Foundation leaders were space industry contractors. Von Braun had brought most of the aerospace companies who had invested in the area to Huntsville's doorstep from elsewhere. As that industry began to wane, the sophisticated development team's efforts turned to more traditional economic growth fare. "Diversification" became the watchword.

Since its early days, Huntsville Industrial Sites and the Research Sites Foundation had been acquiring land for more common industrial development purposes, including land for the (Madison County) Chase Industrial Park. Later those purchases would be supplemented by charitable gifts from the estates of some of Huntsville's most prominent citizens including heiress Jane Knight Lowe and regional banking magnate Beirne Spragins.

Although the HIS and Research Sites Foundation's assets were merged into the UAH Foundation in the period from 1965-1968, the

UAH Foundation's focus continued to be placed on land management for economic development. That practice would continue through the end of the decade, although the University's success and growth slowly began to demand more attention from the UAH Foundation.

The Foundation often met at the downtown Russel Erskine Hotel. Hotel manager Jimmie Taylor exercised the utmost discretion in handling the often "hush-hush" meeting arrangements for this group of community leaders. The group met in the John Hunt Room (after Huntsville's first settler) at the hotel after entering the building unnoticed through the garage entrance.[100]

While the Foundation may have focused its collective efforts elsewhere, individual board members had been active in their support of the University, including soliciting funding for the construction of the second building (Madison Hall) there in 1965.

Beginning in 1966, the Foundation awarded 16 UAH scholarships to Huntsville and Madison County graduating seniors. In 1967, Foundation support for the University was extended to include contributions to the rowing team. The Foundation also appointed a planning committee for the University in 1967. The planning committee was composed of M.B. Spragins, chairman; Tom Thrasher, Louis Salmon, and Phillip Mason. Other committees at the time included the athletic committee, composed of D.C. Boone, chairman; H.M. Rhett, Jr., and F. K. Noojin.

The latter half of the 1960s would see the first changes to the composition of the Foundation Board. On December 20, 1965, Vance Thornton, one of the original members of the 1948 Chamber-created University Advisory Council, died. Less than two year later, in October of 1967, community father Carl T. Jones suddenly passed away. Then in March of 1969, Will Halsey resigned from the board for business reasons.

During this period, two new names were added to the Foundation's Board membership: Alvin Blackwell and William H. Stevens. Their formal appointments would come after years of their having attended the meetings of the Board, and at times their having been (incorrectly) listed as members prior to their actual appointment.

In March of 1969 the Foundation Board consisted of Blackwell, Stevens, Daniel C. Boone, O. Howard Moore, Guy B. Nerren, F. Kenneth Noojin, Harry M. Rhett, Jr., Patrick W. Richardson, M. Louis Salmon, Charles E. Shaver, M.B. Spragins, Sr., and Tom G. Thrasher. Ex-Officio Directors included John A. Caddell of Decatur, University of Alabama Trustee for the Congressional District in which the Huntsville Campus is located; H. Clyde Reeves, Executive Vice President for Huntsville Affairs of the University of Alabama; and Dr. Frank A. Rose, UA President.

Against the backdrop of overall success in UAH's advancement, the local economy faced potentially dark days as spending on the development of Saturn/Apollo steadily waned. Between 1966 and 1969, employment at the Marshall Space Flight Center and in the commercial aerospace sector locally lost more than 7,500 jobs.[101]

Efforts to diversify the Huntsville economy would take on urgency as spending on the space program faltered. The HIEC and the University of Alabama Huntsville Foundation would help to see the community through this difficult time. From 1967–69, the HIEC and UAH Foundation successfully recruited over 4,600 jobs in industries unrelated to the aerospace sector.[102]

A study by the Pentagon's Office of Economic Adjustment in 1974 would credit the efforts of the UAH Foundation and HIEC with avoiding "a potential economic disaster" by organizing an "outstanding industrial development program."[103]

The federal study continued: "The key to Huntsville's success is excellent organization. Many persons are involved in a wide range of programs and *one* organization manages the overall effort." The Huntsville Industrial Expansion Committee maintained sole responsibility for industrial development in the city and county. Other organizations such as the Chamber of Commerce supported the HIEC financially and otherwise as needed, but left the development to the HIEC.

The report credited much of Huntsville's success to its economic development organizational structure. "A community should have only <u>one</u> organization planning and promoting economic growth. When more than one organization in a community seeks industrial prospects, the effect is usually disastrous. A prospect normally turns away from a community if he sees rival organizations promoting industrial development. To him it is a signal that he cannot be assured of full cooperation at a later date if he should locate in the community."

Looking back on the UAH Foundation's role in Huntsville's growth, Research Sites Foundation accountant David Johnston would try to put it into perspective: "I think it's probably one of the top five things that ever happened for the community."

But perhaps more important, according to Johnston, was the comprehensive approach to economic development, of which the UAH Foundation was emblematic. "I think the UAH Foundation is really the byproduct. I think one of the top five things that happened was the use of industrial development bonds, use of the controlled ownership of land to attract industry to Huntsville, and the ability to use that to attract the high-tech clean industry and personal service kinds of industry – rather than a smokestack type of industrial base –

that Huntsville wanted. There was a deliberate attempt to develop this high-tech industry, and to steer clear of the union-type businesses and environmentally unfriendly industries. I think owning the land and perhaps being one of the first regions in the country to have the industrial development bond concept fine tuned so that if industry wanted to come, the paperwork could be worked out in a matter of days. We had the land in hand, and the banks were prepared to provide the financing. If you needed something from the utilities we would have someone at the table, who could answer that commitment, or if you needed the city to approve something, they could take care of it that afternoon. It was just a finely oiled machine, and the UAH Foundation fit into that by being the entity that controlled the land, but it was not an independent player."[104]

Not every economic development project produced success, though. Industrial development leader Guy Nerren recalled that "…in 1965 [industry site consultant] Fantus came in and brought a prospect.…It turned out to be GTE. It was a joint venture between Hoffman Products, a California-based company, and Montgomery Ward to manufacture televisions. We announced their location in Huntsville, and about that time the Japanese invaded the television industry. So they canceled their plans to establish the plant, and it was devastating for us."[105]

Although the GTE plan to locate the plant in Huntsville fizzled, an important opportunity had been born from the effort. The community had produced a labor-market survey while wooing GTE that would prove to be critical in future successful economic development projects.

The labor survey was able to satisfy the "show me" mentality of industry considering the Huntsville region. "Fantus said to us that you have to prove to us and to GTE that you have the [available] labor," Nerren said. "And I remember distinctly one day I received a call from them directing us to have a labor survey to prove that [we] have the numbers of people to support this plant. I, in turn, called Carl Jones and explained the phone call I had just received and that we had to move fast. He said, 'Call an executive committee meeting right now and have everyone there in 30 minutes.' So I did, and they authorized us to go forward and spend the money to do a labor survey."

The labor survey was done in-house by the HIEC per the instructions of GTE/Fantus. The HIEC opened five centers to receive applications including sites at the Armory, City Hall, and a shopping center on South Memorial Parkway. Company monitors were stationed at each location to oversee the application process. Job seekers had to fill out the applications on the spot and were not allowed to take the employment form with them.

The labor survey was a fantastic success. "Over the space of three days, 5,000 people came in to apply for these positions," Nerren recalled. "We printed fliers and hired [advertising agency] Luckie and Forney out of Birmingham to do the advertising for these positions in major publications. They designed flyers that said 'Jobs, Jobs, Jobs,' that became the key word. We had people with the telephone company put them in all the stores and around the county in the surrounding area. This all had to be done in 10 days. We used the Rotary Club and the Kiwanis Club to help us get the word out. It was a communitywide effort. So on the strength of that, GTE said yes, that they would come."

Armed with the labor-study results, the community redoubled its recruiting campaign. Results came quickly. The community's economic development efforts would find their stride in 1966, "a bellwether year for us."[106] Lured in part by the results of the labor survey, Automatic Electric Company decided to locate to the community in 1966. When Automatic Electric opened its doors, it started with 2,500 new employees on the first day.

There was some concern that the labor pool would dry up. "Louis Salmon, the president of HIEC, and I discussed how we would handle the sudden surge in demand for labor, which came about as a result of the survey more than what we did," Nerren said. "It demonstrated the available pool of labor. That was a turning point in Huntsville's industrial development history."

The successful Automatic Electric economic development effort was followed by many more in 1967-1970, including plant openings by

Barber-Colman, Colonial Baking, Dunlop Tire & Rubber Corp., U.S. Corrugated-fiber Box, and PPG Industries. Jobs brought by new industries during this period totaled 4,760.

As the HIEC became more engaged in marketing the community, its members spent less time acquiring property and developing business and research parks through the UAH Foundation. Increasingly, local governments and other entities, including the Huntsville Airport Authority, became the owner and developer of land for industrial development.

The first significant non-Foundation-owned industrial site came with the construction of the community's new airport in January of 1964. The old airport, located just a couple of miles from downtown, lacked adequate property to accommodate needed expansion. A 1,200-acre industrial site some 10 miles from downtown was selected. Though on the outskirts of the county, the site offered excellent industrial development property.

The second significant shift in industrial property ownership came when the Foundation transferred direct ownership in the Chase Industrial Park to the Madison County Commission in July of 1967.

During this late-1960s period, the University of Alabama's Huntsville Campus was experiencing dramatic changes that would ultimately point to its independence from the mother campus in Tuscaloosa. Not all the UA Extension offices would survive this transition to autonomy. Notably, University Extension centers in Gadsden and Dothan did not survive.

Greater independence *was* indeed coming to the University Center in Huntsville, and local leaders would see to its success.

In 1966, the Foundation established its first local endowed scholarship fund --the Samuel Palmer Memorial Scholarship-- adding more student support to that already committed by the UAH Foundation. That same year, UA President Frank Rose announced the Huntsville Campus would officially become a UA branch campus – The University of Alabama in Huntsville. Even as a branch operation though, UAH continued to be tethered tightly to the "mother" campus. "In the early days," UAH Professor Frances Roberts would later recall, "..even an invoice for $2 ... had to go down to Tuscaloosa to be approved."[107]

The Huntsville community, led by members of the Foundation, rallied behind an effort in 1966 to build new facilities for the University. Begun as a graduate studies building, Madison Hall, named in honor of the people of Madison County, was built with $900,000 raised in the community and a $420,000 federal grant. The Foundation assisted the University in both raising and collecting the building fund pledges.[108]

In May of 1968, the Huntsville campus held its first "cap and gown" graduation ceremonies, although diplomas were officially issued in Tuscaloosa. Three UAH construction projects were under way in the spring of 1968 that would double the University's facilities: the Science and Engineering Building, later named in memory of Dr. Harold Wilson, dean of the College of Science and Engineering; the first of four planned phases of a permanent UAH library, which was later named in honor of M. Louis Salmon, one of the founders of the University of Alabama Foundation and its chairman from 1986-1993; and the student union building including a bookstore, cafeteria, lecture rooms, auditorium and student organization offices.

Construction of a general classroom building, to be later named Roberts Hall in honor of the revered local history professor, Dr. Frances Roberts, was scheduled to start in the spring of 1969.[109]

As the decade of the 1960s came to a close, UAH found itself transformed both physically and organizationally. Those changes culminated in a September 4, 1969 vote by UA Board of Trustees to set up the Huntsville and Birmingham campuses as independent, autonomous operations.

But beyond its independence, there seemed little consensus about *what* UAH should become. Several in leadership positions believed that, with the downturn in space fortunes, it should become principally a liberal arts institution. Still others wanted it to focus on technology and science.

It was a time of new beginnings. The University hired its first president late in 1969 when Dr. Benjamin B. Graves was brought on board from Millsaps College in Jackson, Mississippi. He relocated to Huntsville on March 1 and his first day on the job was March 16, 1970.

It was also a time for endings. A few months after Neil Armstrong planted his boots in the gray, dusty lunar soil, the community would bid farewell to its most famous adopted son. Dr. Wernher von Braun accepted reassignment to NASA headquarters in Washington, D.C., effective March 1, 1970.

Just shy of the 20th anniversary of his arrival in Huntsville, the father of America's space program would leave the place he had come to consider home. It was by far the longest that Dr. von Braun would live in one place. Carried on the shoulders of his neighbors and admirers on the eve of his departure, he wiped away a few tears and spoke to the citizens of Huntsville: "My friends, there was dancing in the streets of Huntsville when our first satellite orbited the earth. There was dancing again when the first Americans landed on the moon. I'd like to ask you," he said "don't hang up your dancing slippers."

"I used to be able to say the name of everyone I met on the street – and if they had a dog with them, I knew the dog's name too. Now it's different" - Mayor R.B. "Spec" Searcy.[110]

Alvin Blackwell

Dr. Benjamin Graves

Robert K. Bell

Louis Salmon

Carl Tannahill Jones

Daniel Carl Boone, Sr.

S. Dagnal Rowe

Tom Goodman Thrasher

General Zierdt, M. B. Spragins, and Will Halsey

Clyde Reeves, M. B. Spragins, and Adams Sears

Elizabeth Lowe, Steve Monger, Joe Moquin,
Johanna Shields, and Guy Spencer

Charles Shaver, Alisa Blair, Vicki Wilson and John Wright

Martha and L. G. Rambo

Olin B. and Shelbie King

Sally and Guy Spencer

Susie and Jim Hudson

Kathy and Tony Chan

Judy and Frank Franz

Linda and Mark Smith

Libby and Ray Jones

Gene and Pat Sapp

Amanda and Mike Segrest

Sheryl and Marc Bendickson

June and Derald Morgan

Sue and Roy Nichols

Paula and W. F. Sanders, Jr.

Frank J. Collazo

Peter and Elizabeth Lowe

John Hendricks

Irma Tuder

Elizabeth Lowe and Jean Templeton

William H. Stevens

Chapter Seven: The Foundation Board During The Graves Years

"You can have a great university without having a great city, but I don't think you'll ever have the opposite: you won't have a great city without a great university."
Dr. Benjamin Graves - UAH president, 1970-1977[111]

Huntsville's grasp on success seemed tenuous in 1970.

While the nation celebrated its three and one-half years of fantastic Apollo lunar successes, the downsizings affecting the Marshall Space Flight Center and the local commercial space sector continued. Huntsville ultimately would lose over 12,000 NASA civil service and commercial aerospace-sector jobs in the post-Saturn development era.

The future of the U.S. space program and its ultimate impact on Huntsville seemed far from certain. The last several planned Apollo lunar missions were scrapped and any thoughts of manned missions to Mars were quietly abandoned. The Marshall Center found work converting Saturn rocket elements into the country's first space station, Skylab, which was in service from May of 1973 until the last of three Skylab crews splashed-down on February 8, 1974. The 1975 joint U.S.-U.S.S.R. Apollo-Soyuz mission would mark the last manned space flight for the venerable Saturn launch vehicle and the beginning of a six-year hiatus in the manned U.S. space program.

Even though military spending in the Huntsville economy remained relatively steady during this period (Army employment at Redstone Arsenal increased a scant 1 percent to 11,888 from 1966-1972), the rest of community's aerospace economy took a gut-wrenching ride, lurching from the dizzying highs of the mid-1960s through a painful, almost equally breathtaking decline. MSFC employment during this period went from 7,059 to 5,230. By 1974, the number of Marshall employees had fallen to 4,200 with projections for a further reduction of 1,000 over the course of the next 10 years.[112]

Gains in other economic sectors would mitigate but not completely compensate for job losses in the space sector. Total (nonagricultural) employment fell from 70,855 to 67,744 during this period.[113] In 1973, there were 4,900 unemployed in Madison County, or a jobless rate of 4.1 percent.[114] "There were about 900 vacant houses in Madison County in 1973," and projections were for that number to increase for the next couple of years, according to the Chamber of Commerce.[115]

During this time of economic turmoil, the UAH Foundation kept its sharp focus on what it knew best: Industrial property development. Guided at least in part by the 1960 Fantus study that had mapped the economic development of the non-aerospace sector of the community, the UAH Foundation had acquired prime real estate during a critical time in the community's growth.[116] Had it not been for the watchful eye of the Foundation, the community could easily have missed this once-in-a-life-time opportunity to adequately plan for Huntsville's industrial growth.

In 1970, Huntsville had 10 business, industrial and research parks, most of which had been established by the Foundation, including Research Park with 2,000 acres (owned by the Foundation and managed by HIEC); Madison County (Chase) Industrial Park with 1,000 acres (established by the Foundation and managed by HIEC); Lowe Industrial Park with 500 acres (established by the Foundation); Ditto Landing tract (created by the Foundation) with 300 acres; University of Alabama Tract (established by the Foundation) with 350 acres; Southern Railway Industrial Tract with 411 acres (today known as the Thornton Research Park, owned by the Foundation); Jetport Industrial Park with 1,100 acres; Martin Industrial Park in the City of Madison with 125 acres (owned by the Foundation); the Triana Riverfront Tract with 116 acres; and the Flint River Industrial Tract with 300 acres.[117] These property acquisitions would prove to be essential ingredients in the community's industrial growth for the next 30 years.

Property purchases would be supplemented with substantial property gifts to the Foundation, including a 1973 gift of 1,000 acres of quality industrial property that was bequeathed by UAH Foundation co-founder M.B. Spragins. Mr. Spragins would later be memorialized when the UAH gym was named in his honor.[118]

Spragins' was the largest gift of property that the Foundation would receive. More donations of property and assets would come later.

"For years, the Foundation and Huntsville Industrial Sites were the only publicly controlled organizations with land available for industrial prospects," UAH Foundation President Louis Salmon reported to the local Rotary Club many years later.[119] That began to change in the late 1960s and 1970s as the City, County and Airport Authority began to acquire and develop industrial property. The Foundation's role as the sole industrial property owner was slowly coming to an end.

Economic developers would score an impressive series of industrial recruitment successes in the early 1970s, bringing approximately 1,500 new manufacturing jobs. But those job gains could only partially offset loses in the aerospace sector. According to the OEA report, "The new manufacturing jobs did not fully replace the jobs lost in the space program at Huntsville. There is no question, however, of their importance in alleviating the adverse impact. Without the new jobs in manufacturing, Huntsville's position as a growing regional trade center would have been lost, and the community would have regressed to its former position of a medium-sized country town. Instead, the new manufacturing jobs nourished local business and local government so that growth as a regional center continued as jobs in retail trade, service industries, and local government continue to increase."[120]

In some regards the community was on a roll. The new downtown civic center was under construction in the early '70s, as was an adjacent 200-plus-room hotel. The Russel Erskine Hotel reopened in 1973 following an extensive renovation. But downtown redevelopment was spotty at best, and many storefronts in the downtown area were shuttered.

Several of the region's most successful local high-tech firms had set up operations by this time and were having an important economic impact. By 1977 Intergraph Corp., founded in 1968 by James Medlock, employed approximately 200 people; Space Craft, Inc, (known later simply by its initials, SCI), founded by Olin B. King*, had grown to nearly 1,000 employees; Universal Data Systems, Inc., founded in 1970 by Mark Smith*, employed almost 150, and Dynetics, founded in 1974 by Herschel Matheny, employed slightly fewer than 30.[121] (*Denotes future members of the Foundation Board).

The first edition of the Huntsville/Madison County Industrial Directory, compiled and published by the Huntsville/Madison County Industrial Development Association in 1977, listed 262 companies countywide.

As the importance of its role in acquiring industrial property began to wane, the Foundation came to embrace a new and broader University vision. By 1970, the Foundation's scholarship program had doubled from the 1967 effort to 30 scholarships offered annually to local high school graduates. The Foundation also started acquiring property, not for industry, but contiguous to the UAH campus or otherwise surrounded by the University to allow for the campus' growth.

The City's economic transformation, from virtually all aerospace to broad industrial diversification, was also reflected in the metamorphosis of the UAH campus and its offerings. What had once been essentially an extension of Redstone Arsenal, devoted almost exclusively to the higher-education needs of the government agencies there, was changing.

Much had been accomplished in the 20 short years since the University's Extension office had opened in 1950. During that time UAH had become an autonomous, fully accredited University. Classes that had first been taught evenings in a local high school were offered on a regular day schedule on a campus that had grown to approximately 300 acres with $25 million in facilities.[122] The student body, which had just 137 older part-time students in 1950, had grown to nearly 3,000 in 1970, 35 percent of whom were recent high school graduates. UAH would conduct its first on-campus graduation in June of 1970, with a graduating class of 130.

Despite parsimonious financial support from the State, the University steadily expanded its course offerings into increasingly non-aerospace-related fields. UAH turned its attention to the humanities, social sciences, and health-care fields, to meet the broadening needs of the community.

A statement of purpose developed in 1970 emphasized the "total University," addressing intellectual, aesthetic, social and economic advancement for the region. By this time, the University was offering degrees in 13 undergraduate disciplines. In 1971, UAH would add Ph.D. programs, institute a nursing program, and complete the Humanities building (housing the History, Music, and Art Departments).

Of particular note was the University's growing Division of Social and Behavioral Sciences. Its master's degree program in administrative science taught more than 150 students by 1972. Using part-time faculty borrowed from the Arsenal's well-paid government workforce to augment full-time faculty, the University was able to offer an instructional staff and course of study well beyond its means.

The University also began a medical residency program during this period in the early 1970s. Funded largely by the Foundation's philanthropic efforts, the Foundation acquired the property across from the Huntsville Hospital for the new School of Primary Medical Care program.[123]

Much of this transformation in the University's offerings had been influenced by its new president. Dr. Benjamin B. Graves was hired by the University in late 1969 to be its first president. He assumed office early in 1970.

Graves was a native of Mississippi and U.S. Navy WWII veteran who had come from Millsaps College, where he was president. The new president came with excellent credentials, including a B.A. in political science from the University of Mississippi, an MBA from Harvard University, and a Ph.D. in management and marketing from Louisiana State University. He had taught at the University of Virginia before accepting an endowed chair at Ole Miss.

"Ben Graves gave up a sure thing, the presidency of Millsaps College, which is regarded as highly in Mississippi as Birmingham Southern is in Alabama, a prestigious job and a secure one, for a job with no future and very little history," Pat Richardson observed.[124]

Dr. von Braun had personally helped to recruit Graves to head UAH. "He was the main man in bringing me here…he invited me out to his home on Big Cove [Road], which I later learned was almost unheard of."[125]

Von Braun had plugged the Foundation in making his pitch for Graves to come to Huntsville. "He was the one who told me about the Foundation and how it got started," Graves recalled. "So I knew about it and thought that it was a real plus for Huntsville, and it was a factor in my decision to come here. But I later found out in talking to people [and Foundation Board members] like Alvin Blackwell and John Caddell that the Foundation at that time had a bunch of assets, a bunch of land, but no liquid resources."

Less than a month after Graves started at UAH, the Foundation purchased "a very livable house with about 6,000 square feet"[126] for the new president, paying $69,000 for the 703 Adams Street home.[127] According to Graves, the home had been built by one of Huntsville's pioneers. The mostly nondescript University needed something like that at the time to "hang our hat on," Graves would later observe.[128]

Graves kept close ties with the Foundation group of University boosters. "Sometimes they (the Foundation Board) might decide that we had a quorum out there at dinner one night at my house, and they would have an impromptu Foundation meeting."

In April of 1970, shortly after becoming president of UAH, Dr. Benjamin Graves was among the first group of "outsiders" to be added to the Foundation Board, whose members about this time changed their title to "Trustees." The Foundation also added the UA trustee from the 5th Congressional District and the executive secretary of the UA Board of Trustees to its membership.[129]

When he arrived in 1970, "the campus was a sprawling mess, with very little to tie its disparate parts together," Graves said in a 1989 interview.[130] "The result was that UAH had something like a junior college up there in Morton Hall, and a sophisticated research, space-oriented operation down in the Research Institute. There was nothing, not even a road, connecting the two sides of the campus."[131]

Graves recalled thinking at the time that "UAH's potential, I think, outweighs its problems. Its problems may be exaggerated due to the peculiar way UAH developed."[132]

Although the University had faced dramatic changes in its first 20 years, locals felt it was too constrained by the University of Alabama Board of Trustees. Some felt that the Tuscaloosa-focused board had intentionally thwarted the development of the Huntsville and Birmingham campuses. Others advocated separating entirely from UA System as the University of South Alabama had done. According to Graves, "Every member of the Board of Trustees was a Tuscaloosa graduate. They all wore crimson. They'd never had this (UAH) campus' welfare in mind."

"He [Graves] was looking at a Board of Trustees populated entirely with University of Alabama grads, that he could expect would be highly partial to Tuscaloosa...and they were," Pat Richardson said many years later.[133]

Graves recalled an early retreat with the members of the UA Board of Trustees when Tuscaloosa campus President F. David Matthews proposed several resolutions designed to hobble the development of the Huntsville and Birmingham campuses by limiting on-campus housing, athletic programs and prohibiting post-master's degrees. "We graduate more Ph.D.s in engineering and physics now than either Tuscaloosa or Auburn [University]. [Matthews's] proposals would have been a death blow to this campus." The proposals were tabled.

Even the simple act of choosing names for the system campuses proved controversial. The Board of Trustees charged the presidents of the various University campuses to come up with formal names. Graves and UAB President Dr. Joseph Volker quickly came up with the "University of Alabama in Huntsville" and "University of Alabama at Birmingham" respectively. Months later, University of Alabama President David Matthews, suggested his campus be named the "University of Alabama in University, Alabama." Graves would later complain, "It's the only university in the United States that does not properly identify itself. There's the 'University of Texas in Austin,' the 'University of North Carolina, Chapel Hill,' the 'University of California at Berkeley,' the 'University of California at Los Angeles.' Every other place still tells you where they're located. They should have been the 'University of Alabama in Tuscaloosa.' It still galls me."[134]

"It was a commitment to the future," Pat Richardson said of Graves' vision for UAH. "He had to slug it out, all the way. When Ben Graves came on board he saw to it that the University was set on its feet and on its course as a first-class university"[135] One thing that Graves was not, though, was an engineer, and that would help to broaden the University's academic offerings.

"The first week I was here I got a call from a group of professors up on the north campus; they were primarily from English and history and political science, that kind of group," Graves recalled in a 2001 interview.[136] "They were very serious. In essence, their request was, 'Why don't you get rid of the engineering department down there that's eating up all our money out here? We have all the students up here on the north end of the campus and they have all the money down there.'"

"There was some logic behind that request at the time," Graves added. "It seems silly and ridiculous. But engineering enrollments here were just in a nosedive in 1970. Boeing was pulling out of here. GE had pulled out. IBM was pulling out. This was a gloomy place in late 1969 and early 1970. I told these people, when I finally responded to them, 'I don't want to take any precipitous action. Engineering programs have a way of going in cycles and I feel confident that we'll see that return here.'"

In 1974, the Foundation would elect its first slate of new officers since its founding. Local attorneys Charles Shaver and Louis Salmon were elected president and senior VP - President Elect, respectively. William Stevens was elected vice president; Industrial Development Association (formerly the HIEC) President Guy Nerren was re-elected secretary; and County Tax Assessor O. Howard Moore, was elected Treasurer.

In 1975 the University celebrated its first Silver Anniversary, commemorating 25 years since its first classes were taught. A second Silver Celebration would be celebrated in 1995, marking the 25th anniversary of the first on-campus graduation.

The Foundation began to gain recognition for its support of the University about this time. A UAH publication in 1974-75 stated, "UAH has received substantial support from the University of Alabama Huntsville Foundation. Members of the Foundation's Board of Directors can be credited, either directly or indirectly, for many of the gifts received by the University. And they will undoubtedly play a major role in the future fund raising ventures for UAH. "

"As the only beneficiary of the UA Huntsville Foundation, which is only a decade old, UAH is heir to land valued at more than $2,000,000. This land, located throughout Huntsville and Madison

County, includes all the undeveloped property in Huntsville's Research Park.

"Although its liquid assets have become relatively substantial only during the past two years, the Foundation has given, since 1967, over $100,000 for scholarships and has made contributions valued in excess of $200,000 for other projects including help in purchasing of property for the medical school and support for the UAH athletic program."

Although the Foundation was becoming more closely aligned with the University's interests, it continued to operate independently from the University, conducting most of its meetings away from the UAH campus, at the offices of the Chamber of Commerce and the Industrial Development Association (the new names for the reorganized HIEC) or otherwise in downtown Huntsville. That would not change until the late 1980s.

The Foundation's independence was at times frustrating for Graves. Even the financial situation of the Foundation was closely guarded. "When I first came here, I asked for that [Foundation financial] information, and I couldn't find it anywhere," Graves recalled. "Of course, I knew people who were on the board like Alvin Blackwell, but none of them would tell me how much they had. I knew that they didn't have much in the way of liquid assets, though I knew that they owned quite a bit of property. In fact, I would talk to Alvin

(Blackwell), from time to time and say, 'We'd sure like to do such and such at the University.' He said to come to the Foundation board meeting. I said 'Alvin, you don't have a pot to pee in.'"

The hush-hush nature of the Foundation's property transactions clearly influenced its interest in keeping a low profile in its public dealings. "You know, the men involved with the Foundation had the strangest idea that everything they did had to be kept quiet," former Foundation member Martha Simms Rambo later observed. "Of course, when you were buying land, it was important that everyone not know about it, because the price was going to go up and you couldn't afford it anymore. And that was something the public and press never understood. There are such things as public meetings, but you should not stretch out for the public all the details of your business, and those transactions."[137]

Graves spent considerable time trying to limit University demands on the UAH Foundation. "I spent half my time trying to educate people about the UAH Foundation. They were always knocking on my door saying, 'Let's go to the Foundation and see if they won't do this for us.' I said, 'We don't want to go into that Foundation now. Let's get a corpus big enough to amount to something.'"[138]

By 1977, Dr. Graves decided that he would return to his first love, teaching, and leave the world of university administration. One of his last official acts as president would be to help establish on-

125

campus student housing. His efforts to find funding took him to Washington DC and to the College Housing Authority, which offered low-interest loans to universities.

Although the Washington funding account was tapped out by the time Graves discovered it, he held some hope that more funds might become available. He recalled entering the College Housing Authority offices in the Department of Housing and Urban Development. Graves recalls the scene:

"It was like walking into Grant's Tomb," he said. "The room there was three or four thousand square feet. I saw one man reading a magazine and another twiddling his fingers. There were three or four people there and no one doing anything productive."

When he finally found someone who would talk to him, Graves was told that funds had been exhausted.

Disappointed and disgusted, he went to visit Alabama's U.S. Senator John Sparkman of Huntsville, the author of the College Housing Act, and recounted his visit to the HUD offices. "The next week," Graves said, "we got a telegraph from the College Housing Authority saying that "your application has been approved."[139]

Those funds financed the construction of the Southeast Campus Housing complex, which was built after Graves stepped down from the presidency.

Odds and Ends

The UAH Foundation was a resource for the extraordinary things that happened both to and on behalf of the University. That list included things from the sublime to the ridiculous. A few snapshots from this period in the early 1970s:

- The Foundation owned a couple of hotels over the years – gifts from donors.

- The Foundation owned a lot of property that was intended for industrial development but was used in the interim for growing crops and timber, before being converted to industrial purposes. The Foundation leased its property for cash crops and harvested timber from other property. Future Foundation President and Trustee Ray Jones managed the crop business for the Foundation and Colin Bagwell managed the timber business.

- The Foundation found itself involved in a potential multimillion-dollar housing development after it acquired the 22-acre "Noojin property" in 1971. The Foundation spent $75,000 to acquire the property and considerable time and energy having various development proposals drafted, but ultimately, a developer could not be located. It later transferred the property to UAH.

- The Foundation weighed in on all manner of important matters facing the community, including the location of Interstate Highway 565, in 1973.

- In 1975, the Board authorized $2,000 to support a summer pre-engineering program for black students.

Chapter Eight: UAH Makes The "Wright" Move

Getting to Know You…

On August 24, 1978, the UA System Trustees announced the selection of Dr. John C. Wright to become the second president of UAH. Dr. Wright arrived in Huntsville in time for the fall semester of 1978 and an investment ceremony was held on April 6, 1979. The UAH Foundation had been involved in the selection process through its president, Charles Shaver, who served on the selection committee at the invitation of UA Chancellor Joe Volker.[140]

Wright had been the chief academic officer for the West Virginia Board of Regents. "I was ready to make a move," Wright said in a 2006 interview. "I'd gone to the West Virginia Board of Regents from the position of dean of the College of Arts and Sciences at West Virginia University, and to me it was a way of learning about governance in higher education. So I was prepared for moving back to the campus because I really liked a campus environment more than a board environment."[141]

Unlike his UAH presidential predecessor, Wright had a technical background. He had earned bachelor's degrees in chemistry and mathematics from West Virginia Wesleyan College and a doctorate in chemistry from the University of Illinois. He later conducted post-doctoral studies at the University of Michigan and the University of London.

His professional career included appointments as a research chemist with Hercules Research Center in Delaware, professor and chairman of the Department of Chemistry at West Virginia Wesleyan College, assistant program director for Undergraduate Education at the National Science Foundation in Washington, D.C., and Dean of the College of Arts & Sciences and professor of chemistry at Northern Arizona University. Over Wright's tenure as president, that technical strength would make itself apparent on the UAH campus.

The direction of the University was in flux when Wright arrived. Many in the community supported the idea of a liberal arts college while others believed that the University should be more research oriented. "I think that Ben's [former UAH president Graves] model [for UAH] was more patterned after Millsaps College. It was a really fine undergraduate (liberal) arts education and the quality was there for that," John Wright observed.

In spite of the University's research deficiencies, Wright believed in UAH's unhewn potential. "The mindset of being a research university was not present, and in fact, faculty had not hired-on for that. That was a sort of a tension during my time there, specifically, going about creating research institutes the rationale being that funding is available for research if you are a strong University. And so we built it up while I was there from [not very much]...."

Despite stingy support from the State of Alabama, Wright was successful in building the research program. "When you think about it, the [Alabama] university system really supports a sort of third-rate university education in terms of the money they put in," Wright said. "But you have to be first-rate in research if you're going to compete for funding. And so that creates a tension constantly, because you have to be first-rate in research to bring in those dollars, and the faculty are very competitive in doing that. On the other hand, the State has great difficulty paying for first-rate graduate University education. That is just a tension that's built into the University, and I, with the Foundation's help, probably helped to build that tension in because, [in] the community...a first-rate university education fits in nicely, but it's the graduate education that is the driver for economic activity and it's the driver nationally for evaluating universities."

The first order of business for the Foundation with a new president coming on-board was to find a suitable residence for him as it had done for Dr. Graves. A difference of opinion among the Foundation's Board members about the best solution to the presidential housing situation created at least a little anxiety for the recently arrived Wrights.

"Louis Salmon had arranged for the Echols Hill, [antebellum] Pope-Watts home to be leased by the University as the residence of the president," recalls Wright. "At the time the University had bought a home where Ben Graves lived and where I lived in the first year. And that was the first ticklish situation that I came into, because Joe Volker told me that was what was going to happen, that they were going to lease the Pope-Watts home."

"But I learned that the Lowe home [on Williams Avenue, near downtown] was being left to UAH, and Charles Shaver was their attorney. I went to Pat Richardson, and I probably went to others too, but I remember visiting with him and I asked him what should I do? And he said, 'Let it ripen.' And I said 'How do I know when it's gone rotten?' He said that was up to me to decide. And here I was caught in it, while my wife was busily working with the Watts family [regarding the Pope-Watts mansion], and that was going to be her home. But it all ended up just as smooth as it could be. Winton 'Red' was on the board [UA Trustees]; Louis Salmon was a good friend of Red Blount and they talked and so it went through the board smoothly. Charles Shaver said that we could still have the Lowe home, as the Pope-Watts home was only leased. And like really smart people, and good operators, they worked it all out. It was an interesting experience for me." The magnificent hilltop 1815-era Pope-Watts house, overlooking downtown Huntsville, became the Wrights' presidential residence.

Wright soon discovered the UAH Foundation wasn't your typical university foundation. His first meeting with the Foundation Board came on September 18, 1977.

"A university foundation's typical responsibilities include generating revenue and supporting the university in a broad spectrum of ways including politically through the alumni and otherwise," Wright observed. "While the Foundation did support the University financially and politically, it was how they went about raising those dollars that struck Dr. Wright as unusual.

"To me, it [the UAH Foundation] did not function like a [typical] university foundation. Their focus was not getting income from a benevolent sort of giving gifts and charitable trusts, although there was some of that. Their thinking was more focused upon generating funds for the Foundation from a land investment viewpoint rather than from the more traditional university foundation model. And I don't know that since we were such a new university, that may have been a sort of necessary way of looking at things." To borrow the old E.F. Hutton advertising slogan, "They made money the old-fashioned way, they earned it."

"[The UAH Foundation] was focused very heavily in one particular area (economic development and industrial property management), and they were damn good at that," Wright continued. "Most foundations don't have a mindset of generating income through their own investments. They were sort of like the board of directors for that business and also the Foundation for the University. They were also lead counsel for the development, growth, and improvement of Huntsville, of which the University was a part. But they were interested in operating a specific business and supporting the University and a general improvement in the town. So they were all of those things, and boards are not normally that way. They [university foundations] don't usually care about economic development and local improvement in any real sense," Wright observed.

"I regarded the UAH Foundation members as analogous to a board. They were the powerful people in town, who knew the history of what was going on, and you could clear with them anytime there was a major problem that you needed [help]. The Board of Trustees governed us, but the [Foundation] Board here was the one that I regarded as looking out specifically for UAH. And they were comparable in stature, but just all [residing] in Huntsville," Wright added.

The system of university governance in Alabama was vastly different from Wright's previous experience in West Virginia. "It could not have been more different in Alabama," he said. "In West Virginia you had one governing board over all public institutions in the state, including universities, colleges, and community colleges and I was the chief academic officer. In Alabama you did not have that. The University of Alabama and its three campuses had a board in addition, all of the other Universities and their systems had a board. Each University Board had some control but were not really sure how much."

By this time the University Of Alabama Board Of Trustees did include one of Huntsville's own. Martha Simms (who was previously married to UAH Foundation founder, Pat Richardson, later to become Martha Simms Rambo) was added to the UA Board of Trustees in 1978. "She had gone on the board right before I came to town," Wright recalled. "And it was very useful to have a Huntsville person on the board. John Caddell [of Decatur] had been on the board and I recall that John was the president of the board when I was hired at UAH. So I had good working relations with him, but it was still nice to have someone from Huntsville."

However different the relationship might have been between the University and the Foundation from the traditional model, Wright didn't see it as a negative. "I thought of it more in terms of the growth of the Foundation. They had to evolve into a university foundation; although that's what they were called, they were most unusual. I doubt that there is anyplace else in the United States that has a foundation that was as strong in its existence…prior to the university, where the foundation came along first and then the university. So, just as we were learning what a university was, they were learning what a foundation was. That is the way that I looked at it, rather than 'oh my goodness, they're not functioning like a traditional foundation.' They had to grow into that. They were such a tremendous help in so many of the things that we did, but they did not have the general mindset that a university has."

The Foundation Goes Public

The UAH Foundation model when Wright arrived did present some challenges. As a tightly knit group of friends and fellow investors, the Board hadn't had to face the issue of how they would provide for the permanence of their organization. Wright said that "because the investments in land were so secretive, you could not publicize what you were doing, and they were such a tight group together at the first, that it took some time for them to tend to think of themselves as an ongoing board that needed to provide new membership that would carry it into the future."

The Foundation would pay a price for keeping its activities obscured. The cloak of secrecy that shielded the Foundation's activities from public scrutiny also caused speculation of inappropriate behavior by some of those not connected to its inner circle. A December 1, 1977 article in *The Huntsville Times* brought the Foundation's role in economic development and property acquisition to the forefront. The article, headlined "City Council Eyes Land for New Industrial Park," detailed a plan by the City Council to purchase a "large land area west of the city for a new industrial park for future development."

To the chagrin of the Foundation members, the article laid out a plan to have the Foundation control the land following its joint purchase by the City Council and Madison County Commission.

Within a matter of days, a five-page memorandum was delivered to Peter Barber, the head of the local WFIX radio station, implying that the Foundation had been used by its members for personal gain. The memo ended with a list of 13 questions regarding the Foundation's membership, relationships and activities.

The Foundation Board convened a meeting on December 15 to address the issues raised in the memo. University employees were asked to gather facts about the Foundation's history, explaining its relationships with the Industrial Development Association (formerly HIEC) and the Foundation's evolution from Huntsville Research Sites into the Foundation. The story would also explain that dividends were never paid to any individuals. Over the next few years the Foundation became much more interested in explaining its role supporting the University.

In a report on the University's progress during its first decade as an autonomous campus titled "The UAH Special Report, 1969-1979," the Foundation came out with a fairly detailed accounting of its history. The two-page article traced the Foundation's roots back to the early days of Huntsville Industrial Sites, through its transition with the Research Sites Foundation, and ultimately its metamorphosis into the University of Alabama Huntsville Foundation.

The Foundation took credit for many of its fine efforts that had been largely kept from public view, such as the purchase of the first home for Dr. Graves, the purchase of the Kroger property on Governors Drive for the School of Primary Medical Care, the purchase of the Noojin property, and its support for UAH sports activities including the rowing crew, soccer, basketball and hockey teams.

Nearing the end of the decade of the 1970s, the need to make the UAH Foundation into a self-perpetuating institution was becoming painfully apparent as the number of surviving founders slowly dwindled. By 1979, four of the 12 founders had passed away and another had resigned.

Not long after Wright arrived the Board voted to increase its number of authorized members. At the October 23, 1978 meeting, the Board voted to add six new board positions to the existing ten directors. The existing 10 were T. Alvin Blackwell, Daniel C. Boone, Guy B. Nerren, F. Kenneth Noojin, Harry M. Rhett, Jr., Patrick W. Richardson, Louis Salmon, Charles E. Shaver, William H. Stevens, and Tom G. Thrasher. The Board voted to add local investment house manager W.F. Sanders and original foundation member W.L. Halsey, Jr. to their membership at that meeting. The Board also voted to change its designation from Board "members" to "Trustees."

The personalities of the UAH Foundation Trustees were widely different. They were, according to John Wright, "the most interesting assortment of people that I have ever seen. The main thing that they had in common, that I was aware of, was support and affection for UAH. But if you compare Alvin Blackwell with Harry Rhett, you could not get more opposite. At that time they did not have the Joe Moquin types, but then they began to add the CEOs of high-tech local companies."

The mix of personalities worked well, according to Wright. "Although they were very different personalities, on every issue that I remember they came to a consensus without much difficulty. There were lots of things that were brought up and discussed, so there was lots of exchange of information."

Wright enjoyed a good relationship with the Foundation members. "Charles Shaver was the president of the Foundation, and I lived on Franklin Street and he lived on Locust Street and on his way home and [this was a time when] he wasn't working a full day, he would frequently stop by and we would just chat," Wright recalled. "He was a great guide in trying to deal with the community."

The Foundation was a hard clique to crack in some ways though. "I never considered myself a member of the Foundation," Wright said, even though he was added as a trustee upon becoming UAH president.

The Board would add more new members in 1982, electing Mark Smith, founder of Universal Data Systems (UDS); Teledyne Brown President Joe Moquin, and Coca Cola bottler Robert E. Wilkinson to the Board. The Board would lose two more of its founders in 1979 and 1981 with the passing of O. Howard Moore and D. C. Boone, Sr. Harry Rhett was elected treasurer following Moore's death. In August of 1985, the Board added Ray Jones, the son of Foundation founder Carl T. Jones, and William T. Brooks (with Wyle Laboratories) as Foundation trustees.

John Wright described the challenge of directing the Foundation's attention more toward the development of the university versus the familiar real estate world. "We had to make it clear that Huntsville's goals as a community required a university. I think one of the things that we did was articulate that. And I think that the Board began to understand that those things were linked together. Huntsville could not be what it wanted to be without a university and they were sitting there, playing those two parts of the theme."

Wright and the Foundation Board also faced considerable competition for education dollars from within the UA System. "We had to be careful with that [economic development] theme, because another part of it was the State's investment in education was in the wrong place to build economically. And it was cheaper to build a university in Huntsville than it was to build the infrastructure that we needed all in Tuscaloosa. That was delicate, but the basic story was that this was the place for economic growth in the state and it requires a university, and a university requires an investment."

Clearly that concept had been adopted by the Foundation by 1979 when it laid out the challenges facing the University and community in a UAH booklet: "Our past and present experience has taught us that this region and this University are bound together in many measurable ways. We think our continued prosperity is dependent on this union, and we trust that the best part of our common history lies ahead. UAH provides educational opportunities not available elsewhere in the Tennessee Valley and of the quality that we believe is generally unmatched in most other universities and colleges in this state."

The article set out the UAH Foundation's vision for the University's future: "The growth and maturity of UAH and the needs of the Huntsville area now require further expansion in UAH's graduate offerings, particularly at the master's level, but also in doctoral programs in selected areas." The University's role in research in engineering, physical science, energy and high technology, were touted, as were new programs in the School of Management, allied health fields, and cooperative education. Endowed academic chairs with the support of future private investors were also encouraged.[142] In 1980 the Foundation further amended its Articles of Incorporation to provide that the specific purpose of the Foundation was for the educational, scientific, research and charitable benefit of UAH.

In February of 1979, the Board voted to develop a brochure explaining the work of the UAH Foundation and sponsor a symposium for lawyers, accountants and other professionals to help "sell" the tax benefits of gifts to the Foundation. Slowly but steadily the Foundation's support for the university grew. By 1981 the UAH Foundation support to UAH had reached $168,800.

The University started providing some staff resources to support the UAH Foundation in the late 1970s and early `80s. Although University resources were "thin," it was an important gesture. "We did not have the resources; we were not large enough to really stand up like UAH stands now," Wright said.

Until that time, all administrative functions of the Foundation were handled by the president of the Industrial Development Association, Guy Nerren. According to Wright "He was the hired person who did the Foundation's work."

Nerren's interests had little to do with the University. As Nerren said, "I was not trying to have an influence over how much we gave to the University and whether we supported the salary of someone. It came into play, but I was strictly concerned over how much we can sell the land for. I was hawkish on buying more land. I tried to get as much for it as I could."[143]

By the latter part of the decade of the 1970s, the UAH Foundation saw an opportunity to "recycle" some of its valuable research park property as some corporations downsized their local presence. In 1978 the Foundation was able to repurchase, with UA System Board approval, IBM facilities on Sparkman Drive for $2.5 – $3.1 Million.

The UAH Foundation was increasingly aware though of the University's needs and its role in supporting those needs. By the end of the decade, the Foundation had provided over $190,000 in scholarships to more than 310 students.[144] By 1980 it was annually supporting three UAH scholarships for Huntsville City High School and one scholarship for Madison County High School, for a total of 20 $850 scholarships in the 1980-81 school years. Five regional scholarships from neighboring communities such as Decatur, Scottsboro, Athens, were made available to communities willing to match the Foundation's largess. In 1981 the Board approved $27,000 to support fundraising activities for UAH. At that same meeting, the Board also named a committee to study the staff needs of the Foundation.

Several months later in 1982, the UAH Foundation Board approved funding for a proposed university development office and director. With typical fiscal caution, the Board noted that its policy was to support such commitments only on an annual basis and that it expressly was not the policy of the Board to fund University personnel on an on-going basis. The Board also authorized a part-time Foundation employee to help with paper work at the Chamber of Commerce. For many years, Helen Berisford would act as the bookkeeper for the UAH Foundation. The Board would renew its one-year commitment to the development office in subsequent years.

Without meaning to be pejorative, W.F. Sanders, Jr., may have summed it up best when he observed: "I would have to say that in my own perspective, we began to evolve out of the more mom – and – pop operations [in the late 1980s]. To me the first 10 or 15 years that I was on the Foundation... and I guess I was put on 27 years ago, the Foundation was driven because of the land that it owned."[145]

The Foundation's "parent" organizations, the Chamber of Commerce and the Industrial Development Association, were merged in 1979 - 1980. UAH Foundation Trustee Sanders was the chairman of the Chamber at the time. Some in the volunteer economic development "old guard" harbored concerns that the merger would dilute the economic development efforts of the new organization.

"The last time I saw Pat Richardson, I believe was at the [annual] Coca Cola party" Nerren recalled. "Pat said to me, 'Guy, you ought to have your butt kicked for ever agreeing to consolidate the HIEC with the Chamber of Commerce.' I said 'Well Pat, you know, I respect you for that opinion, but I don't agree that was the wrong thing to do.' I felt like at the time – and I still feel today – that the community is better served by having one organization."

Over the years, as the Chamber of Commerce and HIEC moved its offices, the UAH Foundation had followed in its wake. During the early 1950-60s office locations included the Twickenham Hotel, the Terry Hutchens building, and the Russel Erskine Hotel.

By the mid-1960s, the Chamber had begun planning a facility specifically designed to accommodate its needs. The Chamber, HIEC, and UAH Foundation moved into a new building on the corner of Church and Williams Streets in 1968-1969.

Within a couple of years of the 1980 merger of the IDA and Chamber of Commerce, plans were developed for a new Chamber of Commerce building. As plans for the new building began to take shape, the UAH Foundation in 1982 let it be known that it was interested in office space in the proposed new Chamber facility on Monroe and Church Streets.

City of Huntsville Becomes Primary Developer of Research Park
In 1982, the second major phase of Cummings Research Park was launched. A substantial new parcel of land, exceeding 800 acres, was purchased and master planned by the City of Huntsville. This phase was to become known as CRP West and would elevate development standards in the park to rival – and in most cases

exceed – the quality of planned business parks anywhere in the world.

With the expansion of the park to include CRP West, the full master plan of the park grew to exceed 3,800 acres. The master plan would call for man-made lakes, underground utility service, aesthetic landscape berms, consistent and specific requirements for landscaping, and coordinated management of the outward appearance of all structures constructed within CRP West.

The City of Huntsville also expanded the process of managing the development of the park to include involvement by the actual owners and occupants of CRP, the extended local business community, and a board of business and community leaders appointed by the Huntsville mayor to provide long-term oversight.

Cummings Research Park, first established as a public-private initiative with bright hopes for the future, had become an obvious success. CRP continued to attract substantial investment to the community and would eventually achieve global recognition.[146]

In 1983 the Foundation board made one of its last purchases of industrial property. In January of that year the Board approved a contract for master-planning the development of the Southern Railway property that was to become the Thornton Research Park and on May 16, 1983 the Board "approved $200,000 'pre-payment' to Southern Railway."

In August the Board voted to pay the balance on the Southern Railway property. *The Huntsville Times* picked up on the story in October 1982 disclosing that the Foundation had purchased a 404-acre tract of farm land between Alabama Highway 20 and Madison Pike. Norfolk Southern Corp. donated 40 percent of the tract's appraised value of $3,000 per acre, making the deal a real "bargain purchase," according to Foundation President Charles Shaver. The total tract was valued at more than $1.2 million. Although it lay outside of the city limits, plans were quickly developed to annex the site and zone the property for industrial use.

The Times story went on to peg the Foundation's support for the University at approximately $200,000 per year.[147] This story was followed by a December 18, 1983, Sunday feature story by *Huntsville Times* staff writer Peter Cobun detailing the history of the Foundation and highlighting its role in supporting the new optics R&D effort at UAH. A few months earlier, the Board had approved $100,000 annual support for five years for the new position of Distinguished Professorship in Applied Optics.

The Foundation Rallies to the University's Aid
In the early and mid-1980s, the University was facing a considerable threat from a lawsuit alleging that UAH's development had

furthered racial segregation of higher education in the state. The Foundation weighed in on the Title VI (vestiges of segregation) lawsuit. According to Foundation Trustee Louis Salmon, "The University requested the assistance of expert counsel and the Foundation provided these legal services."[148] The Foundation's share of those legal expenses would reach nearly $1 million before the suit was settled. This expenditure was in addition to the considerable expenses incurred by the UA Board of Trustees.

According to John Wright: "I recall that Pat Richardson felt strongly that they needed legal advice from someone outside of the state who had dealt with that kind of legal situation before. The Foundation was very concerned; they were very protective of UAH. They had the resources and they couldn't think of any better way of applying those resources than to protect UAH. There was even concern that the University would disappear and that it would be assimilated into Alabama A&M [University, also located in Huntsville], as had happened with Tennessee State and Nashville. So there was concern of the gravest kind."

The lawsuit threat eventually ended in a 2006 settlement by the State that put more state money into the historically black Alabama A&M and Alabama State University (in Montgomery) campuses.

The Foundation played an important role providing leverage with the University Board of Trustees on a number of important issues.

"I remember one specific incident," John Wright said. "Congressman [Tom] Bevill had seen the appropriations through the federal government to build what we now call the Bevill Center, a learning facility for the Corps of Engineers. And it was placed on campus, with the facilities that you need for a learning center so that people could come and stay [overnight]. It seemed to me to be appropriate to name that 'the Bevill Center,' especially since he was still the chairman of the [House] Appropriations subcommittee and I thought there might be an opportunity for an encore facility later. The [University of Alabama] Board of Trustees sort of balked at that because he was still a living politician. I remember the Board meeting was coming up in Huntsville, and I mentioned it to some Foundation members."

At the end of December in 1985, the Board voted to send a letter to UA trustees requesting that the new learning and educational center and hotel be named for Congressman Bevill. "That is an example of their behind-the-scenes work. And it just worked beautifully. When the Board of Trustee members came into town, they worked with them, individually," Wright said.

"Congressman Bevill was a good supporter of UAH, but I can't help but feel that [the goodwill gesture of naming of the Bevill Center in his honor] helped with the other $10 million for the [UAH] optics center [that Congressman Bevill later provided]" Wright said. "Later, I think I recall – I'm not positive that it is true – but not much later there was a building on the Tuscaloosa campus that was named for Congressman Bevill."

The Foundation began looking to other states for more traditional models of university and foundation relationships and roles. In 1986, the UAH Foundation met with Mr. Warren Heeman, vice-president for development at Georgia Institute of Technology, who presented recommendations for a model university foundation. Heeman made several recommendations to add structure to the Foundation's activities: (1) set a regular schedule of meetings; (2) change its bylaws to provide for an executive director for university advancement at UAH; (3) elect equal numbers of term members and life members of the Foundation; (4) provide for committees and defined roles of committees; and (5) authorize the nomination of the first round of term membership additions to be approved at the September meeting.

With its "to do list" in hand, the Board quickly set to work. At its September 1986 meeting the Board approved the position of executive director of the Foundation/executive director for advancement of UAH and hired Dr. Thomas W. Tensbrunsel to that post. Tensbrunsel would prove his value to the Foundation in short order. At its next meeting, he announced an anonymous pledge to the University of $600,000 and additional pledges of $188,000, which he predicted would grow to $300,000.

The Board created a nominating committee at its December 1986 meeting to recommend term Foundation trustees, and at its next meeting in January voted to elect the first three term-trustees. Elected were local real estate developer Bob Heath, SCI founder Olin King, and Intergraph founder James Medlock. The foundation also elected a new chairman for just the third time in its history. Louis Salmon became the new president, Tom Thrasher was elected vice-chairman, Harry Rhett was elected treasurer and Chamber president Guy Nerren was re-elected secretary.

In 1987, the Chamber hired its first Cummings Research Park Director, Mickey Mosley.

Ten years after taking the reins at UAH, chemist Dr. John Wright decided it was time to leave the president's office to return to the classroom and assume other administrative duties within the University.

Odds and Ends
- The Foundation received gifts of money, stocks, and real property, including a Beechcraft Sundowner 180 airplane and a car from the Woody Anderson Ford dealership.
- The Foundation was remembered in 1978 when the University dedicated its physical activities building in memory of Mr. M.

Beirne Spragins, naming it Spragins Hall in his memory.

- Members of the Foundation individually helped to get the UAH ice hockey program up and operating. Eventually the Foundation would become directly involved. The hockey team was formed in 1979 and headed up by UAH alumnus Joe Ritch, who served as the unpaid team coach. In 1982 the Board approved contingency funding for the highly successful hockey team program.

- Dr. Joe Dowdle and lawyer Joe Ritch discussed plans to finance a School of Engineering building with the Foundation Board in January of 1983.

- In July of 1987 the board approved $100,000 in funding to support the University's superconductivity program.

Chapter Nine: A New Direction For The Foundation

In 1988, the University hired Dr. Louis Padulo as president, a move some would consider to have been a "wrong turn" for UAH. Padulo's irascible tendencies and imprudent spending would make his tenure at UAH brief. Less than two years after joining UAH, Dr. Padulo would be gone.

In spite of his short tenure, Padulo did bring some important changes to the University. In particular he saw the need to broaden the University's appeal to students on a larger regional and national stage.

In an effort to attract more students from outside the commuting area, Padulo advanced the idea for a residence hall at the Foundation's December 1988 meeting. The Board declined to support the project but did commission a study to quantify potential demand for such housing. Later, when the study failed to document sufficient interest, Padulo balked, asserting that it missed its intended market by only surveying existing students, not those potential students the dorm was intended to attract.

At the Board's February 16, 1990 meeting, Padulo unveiled his revised dormitory plans to the Foundation. This time the trustees agreed to help finance the $6.6 million project and underwrite up to $300,000 of the dorm's first few years of operating losses. With this arrangement the Foundation would establish its preferred method to help stimulate university growth. Using its resources, the Foundation would provide "gap" funding to programs until they could become financially self-sufficient.

A March 31, 1990 *Huntsville Times* article reporting on the dormitory development quoted Padulo as saying, "There are a lot of students anxious to move in." The project would ultimately prove to be a success, though Padulo would not be around to enjoy the moment.

The period between 1988 and 1991 would foreshadow a completely new focus for the Foundation's coming years. During that four-year period the Foundation would see the coming and going of UAH President Padulo and the departure of long-time Foundation Secretary and Chamber President Guy Nerren.

Nerren's letter of resignation was delivered to the Board at its December 15, 1989 meeting. His leaving the Chamber and the UAH Foundation would be the end of an era in many ways. The Foundation's Board minutes from that meeting would note the changing role of the Board. "It now has competition from the City and County in buying and selling [industrial] land," Louis Salmon would note in the Foundation's minutes. "Its primary purpose [now] is to support UAH."

W.F. Sanders, Jr., was elected to fill the vacant position of Secretary of the Foundation resulting from Nerren's departure.

Nerren had been an important cog in the community's economic development machine for nearly 30 years. His primary if not singular interest during that time had been attracting and growing jobs in the region.

The Foundation's relationship with the Chamber began to change not long after Nerren's resignation. The Board immediately indicated its intention to renegotiate its administrative support contract and tenant relationship with the Chamber.

Clearly there had been tension between Nerren and some of the University players. "The University wanted more control [over the Foundation]" Nerren would later recall. "I was dedicated to their not having it. But I was not operating on my own. There were plenty of people on the Board who wanted to keep the distance."[149] But in the end it was Nerren who found himself on the outside.

With Nerren's resignation, the Foundation moved its meetings to the UAH campus, and within a few years it collected its files from the Chamber of Commerce.

With Padulo's departure in 1990, Foundation Trustee and former Teledyne Brown President Joe Moquin was brought on board as the interim president of UAH. Moquin was forced to make historic two percent reductions in faculty and staff salaries. Morale of the faculty and staff was low and frustration was high; unionization was being urged by a group of disaffected faculty and staff.

In spite of all this, Moquin was a stabilizing force in a turbulent time. But Moquin's services wouldn't be needed for long. In less than a year, the University found a new president in Dr. Frank Franz.

Chapter Ten: The Franz Years--Recovery And Growth

In July 1991, Frank Franz, PhD. became the fourth President of UAH. Drs. Franz and wife, Judy, had earlier spent eighteen years as professors of physics at Indiana University, Bloomington, where he also served as Dean of Faculties. They also had spent six years at West Virginia University, where he served as Provost and Vice President for Academic Affairs and Research.

"I did not know very much about Huntsville or Alabama [prior to visiting for the UAH post], but I'd heard a little bit about UAH and their interaction with the community and the Marshall Space Flight Center." Dr. Franz would later recall. "I was very impressed with Birmingham and Huntsville as I flew around the state with John Hicks, the executive assistant to the [UA System] chancellor. The state was totally different from the image they were always fighting."[150]

Franz was likewise impressed with the caliber of people he met during his visit to the state. "When you are dealing with people like Olin King and the other leaders in the community here, and (University of Alabama Board of Trustees Chairman) Yetta Samford, we have a lot of people who are dedicated and visionary."

Franz met with the Foundation as a group. "Louis Salmon was the president of the Foundation at that time. Louis was just an exceptional person," said Franz. "The chancellor felt it important for the candidates for the president's post to meet with the members of the Foundation. In my case it was a special meeting with members of the foundation. I was very impressed with the group. It was clear that the leaders of the community were involved with the University and that was very important."

UAH was facing a financial crisis when Franz arrived.

Insufficient State funding, coupled with substantial over-spending by the Padulo UAH administration had crippled the University. UAH was forced to borrow funds from a sister campus in order to meet a monthly payroll for faculty and staff.

The approaching school year offered no relief. Revenue projections anticipated a three million dollar shortfall and "fund balances" or reserves of the university, were several million dollars shy of obligations. Factors contributing to the fiscal malaise included the heavy debt service incurred for construction of several major facilities, incremental obligations that lacked appropriate funding, and a "responsibility-based" budgeting process that gave budget authority to each division, lacked sufficient oversight.

Franz led an aggressive effort to resolve the immediate emergency and address the long term viability and growth of the University.

- Strong central control of the campus budget was imposed; the ill-advised "responsibility-based" budgeting process was abandoned and tuition revenues were directed to the central campus administration for distribution to campus departments.

- "Obligations" that had not been officially confirmed by the campus administration were cancelled and grant funding was reallocated to help fund University overhead. Incentives were instituted to reward frugality and encourage revenue "enhancements." Tuition was increased.

- A special recurring incremental appropriation of $500,000 was obtained from the Legislature to help address UAH's financial situation with the support of the UA System Chancellor.

- Longer term actions included aggressive refinancing of campus debt; substantial investment to improve both student recruitment and retention; changing the academic year from the term system to the traditional semester system; sale of non-essential capital assets; extensive use of peer university benchmarks in measuring university efficiency and effectiveness, and building and enhancing the physical campus. Confidence and optimism began to return to the faculty, staff, students, and supporters of the University, particularly the members of the UAH Foundation.

Franz recalled that the Foundation's ties to the business community leadership brought him to the Chamber of Commerce often. "When I came to UAH, the Foundation office was at the Chamber. In fact, I remember quite well, going down there and it was, in fact, because the Foundation had contributed to the building campaign for the Chamber of Commerce. The Foundation also had its own accountant [at the Chamber], or the time of an accountant; I recall there was someone specifically assigned to the task."

But those old ties to the Chamber would soon be loosened.

In late 1990, the Chamber hired Larry Waller to be its president. Waller, president of the Cedar Rapids (Iowa) Chamber and a Certified Chamber Executive (CCE), was well respected in national chamber management circles, having served recently as the volunteer chairman of the American Chamber of Commerce

Executives.   Unlike his Huntsville predecessor, though, Waller's background did not include strength in economic development.

The Chamber's professional economic development staff at that time included marketing manager Steve Gollinveaux, who had held the position since 1989. The marketing manager position later became the Cummings Research Park director position. Since much of the Foundation's property interests lay in the CRP, there was regular interaction between the Foundation and the Chamber's marketing manager. The Chamber also employed an assistant for the Research Park director, who managed the CRP property database.

To bolster the Chamber's economic development program, Waller brought Huntsville native Brian Hilson on board in June of 1992, as the Chamber's vice president for economic development. Hilson at the time was the vice president of Birmingham's regional lead economic development organization, the Metropolitan Development Board.

"I did not know of the UAH Foundation's existence until I got here in June of 1992," Hilson recalled, "but I quickly learned that, unique to Huntsville, the Foundation had a role in economic development with the Chamber's responsibility to market the UAH Foundation's land, especially the land that had industrial capability. At that time our [Cummings] Research Park director was also assigned the responsibility of marketing the land and maintaining the

Foundation's financial records, as well as the database, the inventory of land, and all of the details related to the property itself also rested with Chamber staff."[151]

The chamber's staff also included research director Helen Berisford, who kept the financial records for the Foundation as a part of her other Chamber duties.

According to Hilson, the UAH Foundation's decision to locate its meeting space and administrative functions at the Chamber was well thought out. "... [I]t was explained to me early on, by Mark Smith and Ray Jones, W. F. Sanders, Tom Thrasher, and others, that the reason for the existence of this management responsibility resting at the Chamber, rather than physically at UAH was that the UAH Foundation wanted the autonomy to be able to reinvest in land, and they didn't want to sell land and see the proceeds of the sale just simply go to the operations of the University."

But as its property interest waned and the demands of the University grew, the UAH Foundation reconsidered its relationship with the Chamber.

"Well what happened over time was the best of that land was sold off, especially in the '70s and '80s," Hilson observed. "So by the time the early 90s rolled around, what the UAH Foundation had remaining was all of Thornton Research Park [about 400 acres], and a few remaining parcels in Cummings Research Park, a very few of which remain today, and various other parcels around the community. So as the land was sold off the responsibilities of the Research Park director became less with regard to foundation and its property."

The Foundation's investment committee met in the UAH Foundation room at the Chamber on a monthly or bimonthly basis to go over property sales and investment results. As the Chamber's senior economic developer, Hilson was often invited to participate in those meetings.

In 1992, Gollinveaux was replaced by Bill Dean as the director of CRP. Dean had been a successful local banker prior to joining the Chamber. In his new post he worked closely with the UAH Foundation's investment committee managing its property interests.

W. F. Sanders, Jr., would later recall: "You know that probably did not dawn on any of us [the role of the Foundation was not going to be economic development] until perhaps the late `80s or early `90s. It's no question that the Foundation was an early economic development center because of the way these institutions were all tied together, even sharing office space. It might be fair to say that this didn't really come about until Frank Franz came to town, which really hasn't been that many years ago. It's about that time that Guy retired and Frank came to town, and I think Frank began to reshape the role of the Foundation."

Sanders continued, "After Frank came, that was when the restructuring started and that was when the Foundation really started to open up and truly involve all of its members. I mean that everyone on that foundation now is a super community leader. They are very interested in the University and they are real friends of the University, and I think that we have finally put to bed the idea of the Foundation pursuing any large purchases of land. I think we're now concentrating on getting a good value for the property we have left and we're building the endowment."

In 1993, the University would tap one of its own to fill the recently combined UAH Foundation executive director and vice president for University advancement positions. Dr. Sara Graves, a UAH employee, had been working in Washington, D.C., heading up a NASA data and information service system when Dr. Franz approached her about the new position at the University.

"I happened to be in my office at UAH and Frank Franz came in, totally unexpected, and said, 'I need you back at the University and I need for you to consider being the vice president for advancement.' It was not something that I had ever thought about doing. But after a lot of soul-searching, I thought this was something I could help the University with," Sara Graves recalled.[152]

Dr. Graves' background included an M. S. and Ph.D. in computer science from UAH in 1981 and 1984, and math and institutional analysis degrees from the University of Alabama at Tuscaloosa. That very technical background had taken her across the country doing work for a variety of federal agencies including NASA and Department of Defense.

For the two years that she ran the Foundation and University's Advancement Office, Graves focused her considerable energies on raising funds for the University.

She was friends with most of the Foundation members prior to assuming her new role, which helped make for an easy transition and good working relationship. "Well, a lot of the guys I already knew, just being in Huntsville for a long time," Graves said in a 2007 interview. "I probably knew all of the Foundation members pretty well. I was so impressed with how much time those people gave to UAH involvement. And not just on the property part of it, while that was very important to us since that was the basis for a lot of the financial dealings. But they were just interested in a lot of the other aspects of the University."

At her first meeting with the Foundation in January of 1993, Graves thanked the Foundation members for their support and gave an overview of the Advancement division which included development, university relations and alumni affairs. With friendly candor she also noted an obvious, if painful, transition that would soon be required: the Foundation trustees would be asked to play a more active role in soliciting gifts for UAH.[153]

The University soon kicked off a major fundraising effort through the University's Silver Anniversary Celebration. "One thing that UAH had not done very well was to raise funds. So we launched a very large fund-raising campaign called the Silver Celebration," Graves recalled.

The five-year goal of the campaign was to raise $10 million, the bulk of which would go for University scholarships. "The Foundation members were very involved in that. They were very instrumental in helping launch it, as were members of the University of Alabama Board of Trustees," Graves said.

Dr. Graves would turn to one of UAH's most prominent graduates, Discovery Channel founder John Hendricks to head up the fundraising effort. "(John) was quite involved in the Silver Celebration. Frank and I met with him and he agreed to be the chairman, and I think that since then, he has been added as a Foundation trustee. I think it was a very good move by the UAH Foundation to incorporate people [into the effort] who weren't just living in Huntsville."

Sadly, the Foundation would lose one of its most ardent leaders in 1993, when Foundation Chairman Louis Salmon passed away. Efforts were soon underway to name the UAH Library in Salmon's honor. By the end of 1996, less than three years after the effort had begun, the Foundation's fundraising campaign in support of the Salmon Library was slightly over halfway to its goal of $1.1 million.

Local Attorney S. Dagnal Rowe would be elected to fill Salmon's Board seat. "I think that when Louis died, (former law partner) Pat Richardson promoted my candidacy, and, boy, was I flattered to be a part of that crew," Dag Rowe would later remember.

"In my opinion, There are damn few ordinary people who have been on the UAH Foundation Board. It has been a remarkable group of people in terms of their civic leadership, as well as the success of their own careers. And so when I was asked at the age of 45 to serve on the Foundation Board I was super-flattered. And I attribute that largely to Pat [Richardson]. He was the chairman of the nominating committee as long as I was on the Board. And I imagine he had been the chairman of that committee for a long time."

Former Wyle Laboratories executive Bill Brooks would take the reins at the Foundation following Salmon's death.

When Helen Berisford retired from the Chamber in 1994 "that was the last domino to fall" regarding the Chamber's close affiliation with the Foundation, according to Hilson. "There was a push at that time …to move the Foundation to campus. It would be closer to them, they would hire a development director, who would manage property sales, and obviously UAH would have its hands on the finances of the foundation."

President Franz saw the Foundation's role changing. "I think that in the early days, and partly during my tenure there was a tendency by some of the members of the foundation to view themselves as more of a landholding operation and an economic driver in the community to do that. …the evolution was that it became much more a support arm using that land, and that landholding operation to become much more of a support arm for the University.

Helen Berisford had managed the Foundation's books since the 1960s. "There was a sense of confidence that the Foundation members had with Helen managing the books," Brian Hilson recalled. "There wasn't a lot of activity, and it was sort of a sideline for her here and it took maybe 10 or 15% of her time. And it just sort of worked out. The motivation for the Chamber in doing that all along of course was the fact that that property was strategic to our marketing efforts. It became less strategic as it was sold off, but it was important to have that."

The financial implications of the Foundation pulling out of the Chamber weren't considered to be significant. "At that time, the

Foundation compensated Chamber of Commerce for the service of marketing the land, managing the books, managing the property records, everything for around $15,000" Hilson later observed.

UAH President Franz would later recall the relocation from the Chamber, "First of all it (UAH) took over the accounting function for the Foundation. And when the Foundation gained confidence in the University's ability to manage its financial affairs...and remember that when I came to the University it was in bad financial shape but when the Foundation had that confidence, and not just me, but in the University's ability to manage its financial affairs and they saw the advantage in having the entire accounting staff at the University...they turned the books over to the University."

As the University demonstrated its effectiveness in managing the affairs of the UAH Foundation, it felt more comfortable putting all its fundraising efforts into the UAH Foundation.

"At one time, I believe in the past, there was a competition between the University and the Foundation. That's silly, that doesn't make any sense at all" Dr. Franz later recalled. "At the same time, the University stopped urging people to make donations to the University rather than to the Foundation. It didn't make any difference, in effect, we would prefer the people have donations made to the Foundation and for the Foundation to hold the money and make donations to the University. So that was a further transition. Likewise the University has pooled a lot of its fund raising activities with the Foundation. It doesn't make any difference now with you give money to the Foundation or to the University it is still going to end up going to support scholarships and supporting things that are going to help the university move forward."

The next Foundation minutes record a meeting on November 10, 1995. By this time, Dr. Graves had become the head of UAH's Research Center for Technology. "We had both agreed, Dr. Franz and me that we would like to set up a research center in information technology. So after I left the VP slot, I really went back to more of my roots. And we set up the center, and the Board of Trustees sanctioned some of the centers as Board of Trustees centers, and this is one of them," Graves said.

Barrett H. Carson was selected to become the new University vice president for advancement and secretary and director of the Foundation. "He was a person – and my view is based on what I've read – who was the first guy that really understood advancement [fundraising] from a broad perspective, having been somewhere else," Foundation Director Dr. Derald Morgan would observe. "He came here from Virginia Tech, and had experience in running a development organization. I must say that having read many of his reports, he is the classical, old-fashioned development person. Unfortunately there were apparently things that he did not do, but he did others well. It is very interesting to read the file on Barrett because he was a good one. He clearly was the consummate development professional coming up from that route and having that experience." Unfortunately Mr. Carson's departure to become Vice President for Advancement at Georgia Tech gave him less than two years tenure at UAH.

The Foundation received several substantial gifts in 1996 including a building from SCI, Inc. and $150,000 from Mr. and Mrs. Larry Durkee. The Durkees' contribution pushed their total giving to the University in excess of $500,000, making them the third-largest donor in the history of the University at the time.

At the Foundation's March 4, 1996 meeting, the relationship with the Chamber was once again discussed, including the Foundation's $20,000 annual contract with the Chamber. Of that amount, $19,000 was for secretarial duties, land management, and property sales and $1,000 for the facilities and janitorial services at the Chamber. Mr. Brooks said "he believed there had been six different people in the secretarial/administrative position since his involvement with the Foundation, leaving no continuity. Those positions have since been moved to the University."

As an alternate means of continuing its support of the Chamber, the Foundation proposed a commission relationship with the Chamber for the sale of the Foundation's industrial property. But Hilson,

who had become President of the Chamber, quickly declined the
offer.

"Ray (Jones) called me and said he would like to put the Chamber
on a commission basis arrangement to sell the land. I immediately
said that we could not do that. I said that while it might be
financially attractive to us, the mere appearance that there may be
some impropriety with the chamber selling foundation land for
commission, when that land is in effect competing in the market
with the Airport Authority's property. I went back to the time, when
I know Guy Nerren and (former airport authority director) Ed
Mitchell were butting heads over the appearance or the perception of
issues like that and I didn't want that to happen. So I told Ray that
we couldn't do it. I told him why we couldn't do it and I
immediately called Rick Tucker (the head of the Airport Authority)
and told him that discussion a taken place and I wanted him to know
where we stood in case he heard anything otherwise, he was wrong"
Hilson said.

"You can imagine over the years how financially lucrative it
would've been for the Chamber to have sold ... (industrial sites), on
a commission basis... But we didn't do that and I'm glad we didn't
do that" Hilson recounted.

The Foundation minutes from March of 1996 would reflect the
discussion saying "The Chamber felt if they accepted this proposal

(to be paid on a commission basis for the sale of industrial property), other organizations in the community would expect the same arrangement so the Chamber declined the proposal and the Foundation has notified the Chamber we will handle land dealings differently."

The nominating committee of the Foundation, chaired by Pat Richardson, proposed that the incumbent officers be re-elected, and that motion was approved at the March 1996 meeting. The committee noted the passing of founding Trustee Harry M. Rhett, Jr. with a resolution. Rhett's death would reduce the number of original Foundation members still serving to three.

When the Foundation reconvened three months later for its next meeting, a new slate of Foundation officers was proposed. At this meeting the nominating committee proposed businessman Ray Jones for chairman, stock brokerage manager W.F. Sanders, Jr. for vice chairman, oil distributor Guy Spencer for secretary and Steve Monger for treasurer.

Jones clearly understood the Foundation's role to support the University. "I think it has been very advantageous to the University to have this Foundation, because we're not only able to support it financially, but if you'll read the members of our Board, it looks like a Who's Who, with the Mark Smiths and Roy Nichols and everyone else. A lot of things that you won't find on paper are those times that those people used their personal influence to help the University. If they [UAH] found themselves in a tangle with someone either at the city or the state or even the federal government, then the Foundation members were right there to help."

The minutes of that meeting reflect Jones' deep involvement in the Foundation's business dealings. In the three months since the last Foundation meeting, the executive committee including Jones, had met three times to discuss three land development efforts totaling $25 million.

More than the leadership of the Foundation had changed. It also began to look for opportunities to improve its business practices and policies. A change in investment policy adopted that year allowed up to one-half of the Foundation's current investments to be placed into managed endowment funds. The Foundation transferred $850,000 in cash and investments into the University of Alabama System Pooled Endowment Fund in June 1996.

UAH's President Franz said, "And another transition occurred – that was how the Foundation invested its money. That which was not in land was in CDs and things of that sort around the city. So in this evolutionary process... a substantial portion of that money was moved into equities. And then also, finally, we took advantage of the Pooled Endowment Fund of the Alabama system, which has had better rates of return. Ray Jones and Mark Smith and others had a big role in that change. And so, as I look back on it, it was... actually rather quickly that the Foundation gained confidence in the University and realized the benefits of having a very close association."

In June of 1996, new Foundation Trustee Dr. "Tony" Chan presented a gift of $400,000 to the University. Plans to name the Auditorium in the Administrative Science Building in honor of Dr. Chan's father, Pei-Ling Chan, were also announced.

In late 1997, heiress Jane Knight Lowe bequeathed her $1.25-million home at 210 Williams Avenue in Huntsville to the Foundation. Initially the organization considered selling the property; however, it soon learned that Mrs. Lowe intended for the property to be *used* by UAH for official purposes.

The Lowe home dated to 1902 and was designed and built by the Herbert Colwell Company in Chicago. The 7,000-square-foot house was shipped to Huntsville by rail in numbered parts to be assembled.[154] According to Foundation Trustee Mrs. Martha Simms Rambo, "It was a method frequently used in that era."

Mrs. Lowe's decision to donate the house to the University was "appropriate in that Jane was always interested in education," Mrs. Rambo added.

Initial estimates projected that $700,000 would be needed to restore and furnish the home. Several Foundation committees were set up to oversee the project: Mrs. Rambo chaired the decoration/furnishings committee; Mr. Olin King chaired the architectural/structural committee; and Dag Rowe chaired the fundraising effort.

The renovation would be completed nearly four years later and cost slightly over $650,000 with all of the needed funds having been raised by the Foundation. During the restoration it was decided that the property would be reserved for use by the University and patrons who had contributed to its restoration.

By August of 1997, Foundation Director Barrett Carson would be gone. The Foundation soon saw the coming and going of two other directors before appointing Dr. Derald Morgan to fill the post. Morgan joined the staff in April of 1999 as the new Vice President for University Advancement and Executive Director of the UAH Foundation.

Morgan had previously been dean of engineering at New Mexico State University and had first come to Huntsville to consider the engineering dean position at UAH. Franz later invited him to apply for the advancement vice presidential post.

Morgan had spent the last 14 years with New Mexico State University, and before that was the head of electrical engineering at the University of Missouri - Rolla. While at NMSU he developed an impressive record soliciting grants, contracts and gifts for the College of Engineering, growing those grant and contract activities from $1 million per year to over $30 million per year of expenditures and private gift funds from zero to $7 million the year he left.

Morgan saw much similarity between the deanship he had held and the UAH advancement and Foundation jobs. "The dean's job is alumni relations, getting money for his college," said Morgan. "Where do you get that money for your college? There are five sources: state money, federal money, corporate money, foundation money, and alumni and friends' money. So realistically, a good dean does all of those things. I think a lot of people believe that a dean just sits there and thinks about curriculum. While it is probably at a lower level than the president, basically a dean is a small center of advancement."

"I had lunch at the [private] Heritage Club with probably…18 or so of the Foundation Board members. They were certainly a high-level group of people interested in supporting the University. At the meeting were Ray Jones, Jim Hudson, Mark Smith, Tony Chan, Alvin Blackwell, W. F. Sanders, Jr., and Olin King among others. It was a group of people who continue, in fact, to be key to supporting the University."

Upon taking the post, Morgan discovered that the records for the Foundation were "spotty" at best. "In terms of procedures and policies and processes...Things needed to be changed. Both the University and Foundation parts of the equation needed attention at the executive-direct level," said Morgan.

His knack for organization and fundraising quickly won him praise from the Foundation members. "Derald Morgan has been a real find for Frank [Franz] and the Foundation... a real pro. He just knows how to do it. I guess we have had 10 development officers in the time I've been on the Foundation Board and none of them have been able to organize and involve the members of the foundation the way this man has," W.F. Sanders observed.

In Morgan's very first year, giving to the UAH Foundation and University topped $10 million and has been running between $4 and 6 million each year since.

His work also brought accolades from Franz: "Derald Morgan has done an outstanding job. He's worked very hard with Mark Smith, Gene Sapp, Olin King, John Hendricks, Peter and Betsy Lowe and the other members, developing the President's Council. Once again, it's foundation members helping to support the University."

Sanders would echo that assessment: "One of the great things that [Morgan] did is that he has helped develop this President's Council. And it's a pretty simple thing. You contribute at least $1,000 a year, you are invited to a very fine dinner once a year, and you are involved in things on the campus. You are brought into the campus life. Gene Sapp had been the head of that organization the last couple of years, and I believe we [initially] had maybe 200 members. That's $200,000 a year, of course. I remember when we didn't raise $200,000 *in a year* for the Foundation. But now we've got 399 [Council members], and we are soon to have our 400th member. That's $400,000 a year. But of course, we take in millions every year now."

Another change instituted by Morgan was a published annual report for the UAH Foundation. Many of the Foundation's achievements and contributions to the University that might have otherwise escaped notice were given their due recognition. The first year's annual report bears a memorial to civic leader and oil distributor Tom Thrasher, who died in December 1999 at the age of 83. Thrasher was credited with having the vision to position the fledgling University extension office so that it could eventually become the independent and vibrant University that UAH is today. "In the 1950s, after the tract of land now known as the UAH campus was purchased by the Huntsville City Council, Tom was a member of the team that helped establish UAH"[155] the tribute states.

179

In 2001, the UAH Foundation approved Dr. Franz's request to underwrite the cost of a new residence hall, estimated at $8 million. Franz recalled the significance of the Board's support for the residence hall project in a 2006 interview. "We couldn't create a business plan which showed the new residence hall being immediately filled" with students. "We could not build on experience and say that with certainty... but we felt sure that it would fill within two or three years – 'if you build it, they will come.' The Foundation enthusiastically said 'Yes we believe that too,' and so we built it and they came."

About the same time, Chairman Ray Jones disbanded the Foundation's investment committee and created a new campus planning committee. With so much of the Foundation's assets invested through the University's trusts, there had been little for the investment committee to manage. The Foundation would later establish a finance and audit committee, at Morgan's urging, to evaluate and approve the budget, manage local investments, and oversee the proper operations of the Foundation's business. Per federal guidelines this committee was established as an independent audit committee was given the power to hire without further board approval the necessary professional services to evaluate the actions of its members and director should such become necessary.

The planning committee, on the other hand, had much to do. UAH needed a Master Plan for its SACs accreditation review. Working in concert with UAH Vice President Pinner, the UAH Foundation planning committee joined forces to develop and implement a Master Plan. About a year after establishing the committee, Chairman Marc Bendickson and his committee initiated work with the UAH team on a campus master planning activity.

In 2003, the Board took the planning effort public. UAH Foundation Executive Director Morgan was quoted in *The Huntsville Times* as saying that "[the Foundation would share] the cost of a long-range study to help decision-makers chart a course for traffic, new building, more land and other improvements. As a blueprint for improving the campus and making it more attractive to students, the 25-year plan will study everything: traffic patterns, landscaping, the overall "look" of the signs and facilities, the acquisition of more land, and where new building should be located."[156]

From the time that the University campus and Research Institute facilities were first established in the early 1960s, it had been apparent that a housing subdivision lying between the two would need to be removed to allow for the development of the University. This housing development was known as the Sanderson subdivision. Early in the University's development, the UAH Foundation adopted a policy of purchasing these houses as they came available. By the end of 1990, it had acquired 13 of the 35 houses in the neighborhood. In the later 1990s ownership of these houses was transferred to UAH. By February of 2004, UAH owned 27 of the homes, and three years later the University would own all but four of the 35 houses. Thirteen of these houses had been removed by 2007, with more slated for removal.

The campus Master Plan was unveiled in *The Times* on February 7, 2005. The plan called for a series of improvements to make the campus "more student-friendly." Features in the first five-year phase included the completion of the second North Campus Residence Hall; the $60-million-plus Richard and Annette Shelby Center for Science and Technology; a "gateway" to the campus from traffic artery Sparkman Drive; improved parking facilities; new fraternity and sorority houses; new athletic and practice fields; and sidewalks, landscape lighting and sign improvements to better "connect" areas of the campus.

"Longer-term goals include additional laboratories and classrooms; a performing arts/cultural education center; a new student center; a new liberal arts building; and if possible, modifications to Holmes Avenue," a main road cutting through the heart of the campus.

The Master Plan was intended to address one of the biggest challenges the University has ever faced. The institution lacked many of the things that are found on other traditional residential campuses. It needed bicycle paths, walkways, on-campus residences, green spaces and gathering areas to complement and enhance the student experience at UAH.

The long-range plan addressed this complicated challenge in some very concrete ways. In fact, several of the projects included in the five-year plan had already been jump-started by the UAH Foundation by the time that the plan was released.

Funding for the second north campus residence hall had been approved by the Foundation at its February 2003 meeting. Pat Richardson made the motion to proceed with the second hall before the mortar on the first residence hall had fully cured. The second hall would be built using the Foundation's pledge of support and a $1 million contribution by Foundation trustee John Hendricks.

Franz recalled the leap of faith required of the UAH Foundation to support the second north campus residence hall. "Building the second north campus residence hall was even more of a stretch," the 12-year UAH president said, "and the Foundation agreed to support it through its first years. There are few things more critical than having those two additional residence halls. They transformed the nature of the campus, and the UAH Foundation underwrote that change.

The need for funding to help build fraternity and sorority houses were discussed at the same time. At the 2004 President's Council

Dinner, Franz indicated that one of the major next steps on the list of priorities for the campus would be the construction of fraternity and sorority houses. By October of 2004, the first donor had agreed to contribute the funds needed to begin construction of the fraternity and sorority houses.

Franz saw the Foundation members' donations to help build the Greek housing as another critical step in the University's development. "Susie Hudson [wife of trustee Jim Hudson] made the first donation and... Mark and Linda Smith made the second donation bringing the total to $2.5 million with the University matching this amount and owning the houses." Putting the donations into perspective, trustee Rowe said, "The effort to build a fraternity and sorority row, what does that do? It makes for a traditional campus, where people come as freshmen and graduate and perhaps they go on to graduate school, and they have an emotional attachment to the University, and that will help."

The Nature of the UAH Foundation Continues to Evolve
"The Foundation has been in the real estate business since day one," Rowe observed. Some of the glamour and some of the excitement and some of the connection with the past with these multimillion-dollar real estate deals are going to be behind us. We're going to be like Smith Barney: we're going to have to get money the old-fashioned way – we are going to have to beg for it. "That is a change that is a coming. And the Foundation will face unique

challenges as a young university in raising those funds. Since most traditional support for a university comes from wealthy older alumni, UAH is at somewhat of a disadvantage. According to Rowe, "We don't have many 80-year-old alumni, 70-year-old alumni, or even 60-year-old alumni."

UAH's overarching goals during the Franz tenure were to expand and diversify the Universities research base; to make UAH a more welcoming, more attractive, more effective university for students, faculty, staff and friends and to transform UAH from a predominantly part-time transient commuter campus to a student-oriented traditional research university of excellence, a destination of choice rather than one of convenience. Great progress was made and as of fiscal year 2006-2007:

- The undergraduate student body had become predominately full-time, with more than 85% of undergraduate instruction now being delivered to full-time students.
- Instruction, as measured by credit hours delivered, was at an all time high.
- UAH's student body had become substantially more cosmopolitan and diverse. By this time UAH students came from almost every county in Alabama, from more that 40 other states and form more than 80 other countries.

- The African American proportion of the undergraduate enrollment had grown to 15%.
- UAH's research productivity had continued to expand to more than $70 million in research awards per year. UAH now led all Alabama universities in the annual amount of research performed in the combined disciplines of Engineering, Physical Science, Computer Science and Environmental Science.

According to Franz, the future role of the UAH Foundation should be focused in three primary areas: First, the Foundation needs to "encourage people of wealth and their associates and friends to 'adopt' the University. We have a very small endowment for scholarships. The UAH Foundation has helped us to build it, but still it is quite small compared to where it ought to be. We need friends telling friends to remember us in their wills."

Second, the UAH Foundation members should "bring their personal influence to bear at various times to assist us. That and providing us with a strong community voice in favor of supporting the University and what the University contributes. The late Mark Smith and Olin King co-chaired the President's Council of the Foundation and have been eloquent when they talked about the contributions the University can and does make to the community, especially the technological community."

Lastly, the Foundation's challenge is to include the next generation. "We are always trying to make sure that we have the door open to new leaders in the community, to those who really help to make Huntsville/Madison County what it is," concluded former UAH president Franz.

Chairman Ray Jones sums up the Foundation's responsibilities this way: "The purpose of the UAH Foundation is to support the University. We don't have any other goals. As far as the goals of the Foundation, it is to do those things better. We will do all that we can to encourage people to support the UAH Foundation and the University. We don't have any numbers in mind, we will bring the very best that Huntsville has to offer. And we will press for the University with whatever that entails."

The Ray Jones Era

Ray Jones, an Auburn graduate and local businessman and farmer, has led the UAH Foundation since 1996. His leadership and steady hand at the helm has produced some of the most amazing results ever seen by UAH. Jones continues to work tirelessly for the betterment of UAH and the expansion of the capabilities of the UAH Foundation to serve UAH and its faculty staff and students. Jones as well as many other business and civic leaders of the area recognize that von Braun was right, it is not the land, the water, the roads or even the weather it is the "brain power" that drives the growth and improvement of the community. UAH is central to the community's development of brain power.

Under Ray Jones's leadership, working closely with the UAH President and Vice Presidents of Advancement and the Executive Directors, the UAH Foundation Trustees have accomplished an impressive list of achievements unparalleled in the history of the university. The UAH Foundation and its individual members played major and important roles in the realization of the following projects:

1. Olin B. King Technology Hall with its associated land was transferred by gift/purchase to UAH and UAH Foundation, and then ultimately to UAH from the SCI Corporation and in part from the successor Sanmina-SCI Corporation. UAHF Trustees Olin King and Gene Sapp championed these transactions.

2. Shelbie King Hall was transferred to the foundation and then to the University through a gift/purchase from UAH Foundation Trustee Olin B. King and the building was named in honor of his wife Shelbie.

3. Robert (Bud) Cramer Research Hall was made possible by a gift/purchase from former

UAHF Trustee Robert Heath. The government contributions for the remodeling and additions to the building were championed by Congressman Bud Cramer, Senator Richard Shelby and State Senator Tom Butler.

4.	Development of Frank Franz Hall, first known as the North Campus Residence Hall I, was underwritten by the UAH Foundation.

5.	North Campus Residence Hall first known as North Campus Residence Hall II, was supported in the same way as the first North Campus Residence Hall by the UAH Foundation and additionally by a four-year support gift from former UAH Foundation Trustee and graduate of UAH, John Hendricks and his wife.

6.	Fraternity and Sorority Row was made possible by Susie Hudson, wife of UAH Foundation Trustee Jim Hudson and UAH Foundation Trustees Mark and Linda Smith.

7.	The vision to purchase the Sanderson Subdivision houses was initiated by the UAH Foundation through their early purchases of 13 houses and subsequent gifting to UAH. UAH continued the purchase of houses and operated them as rental properties until today

31 of the 35 houses were owned by the UAH. Many have been moved or are in the process of being moved.

8. The University Fitness Center was built.

9. Renovations and Expansions made possible by Federal, State and University funds have included Spragins Hall (named for UAH Foundation Trustee M. B. Spragins), Southeast Housing, Salmon Library (named for UAH Foundation Chairman Louis Salmon) and the University Center.

10. One of many new facilities that have also been funded by Federal, State and UAH funds as a part of the Master Planning process, in which the UAH Foundation played a major role, is the Richard and Annette Shelby Center for Science and Technology.

11. The formal campus entrance off of Sparkman Drive and the associated lake complex.

12. The Intermodal facility that is under construction.

13. Site preparation for the Baseball/Softball Complex and associated parking was made possible using soil provided by one of the Foundation's members.

The assets of the Foundation have risen to $53 million during the Jones' years of leadership as Chair of the UAH Foundation. The vast majority of the land holdings has been sold or is under contract for sale. The past 10 years has seen the fundraising from private gifts exceed the total value of all previous giving to the Foundation and UAH. The Foundation has continued to evolve as a major source of financial and community support for the continued development and enhancement of the educational and research opportunities afforded the nation, the state and the region by UAH.

Board Appointments
The UAH Foundation has counted among its number some of the Huntsville/Madison County community's most effective leaders. They have been visionary in their leadership and tremendously generous with their time and their gifts. A list of all who have served the UAH Foundation is given in Appendix A.

For the first 30 years that the Board and its predecessor organizations existed, only 24 people would be counted as members. Twelve of those were founding members.

As the Foundation moved out of its "mom and pop" phase, it began to broaden its reach across the community and include more people. Board appointments prior to 1990 have been listed chronologically in the preceding pages. Board appointments made in later years are listed here.

In December of 1990, real estate developer Bob Heath and then-SCI, Inc. Chairman Olin King were re-elected to second four-year terms on the Board. Nichols Research co-founder Chris Horgen and Redstone technician Larry Durkee were also elected to four-year terms.

In 1992, the Foundation added residential property developer Peter Lowe to its board as an ex-officio member upon his selection as the new local member of the University of Alabama System Board of Trustees. Lowe, coincidentally, is married to the daughter of the late UAH Foundation founder Carl T. Jones. Guy J. Spencer, Jr. was added 1993-95.

At its March 1995 meeting, the Foundation re-elected Chris Horgen and Larry Durkee to the Board and elected Olin King a lifetime member. The Board also created a new category of Emeritus member and named Will Halsey to this new category. Local orthopedic surgeon Dr. J. Kendall Black, Jr. and aerospace industrialist Russell G. Brown were added to the Foundation as new Trustees later that year.

In March of 1996, Boeing's Bob Hager was made a Board member emeritus and local banker and former Chamber Chairman Steve Monger was added to the Board. The committee noted the passing of founding Trustee Harry M. Rhett, Jr. with a resolution. Rhett's death would reduce the number of original foundations members still serving to three.

The Foundation Board added Dr. Chia Hwa (Tony) Chan to its membership in June of 1996.

The year 1997 would mark the last meeting of the board that Alvin Blackwell would attend. Although he remained a member of the Board, failing health prevented him from attending future meetings.

In mid-1998, Jim Hudson, the founder of Research Genetics and community volunteer Betsy Jones Lowe were added to Foundation Board. As her term on the University of Alabama System Board of Trustees was drawing to a close, Martha Simms Rambo was elected to a full term on the Foundation Board. Mike Segrest, son-in-law of Foundation patriarch Tom Thrasher was also elected to the board that year. It would be an unofficial passing of the torch as Thrasher's failing health would prevent him from attending future meetings.

In 1999, Larry Durkee was elected a lifetime member of the Foundation and Dr. Black, Russ Brown, and Sid McDonald of Arab, Alabama, were re-elected, as were Dr. Chan and Mr. Monger a few months later.

New members John Hendricks and Dr. Marc Bendickson were elected to the Board in 2000 and Roy Nichols was added in 2001. After many years of dedicated service, trustees Horgen, Spencer and Noojin would rotate off the Board. In 2001, Alvin Blackwell was elected Trustee Emeritus, Dag Rowe was elected Trustee for Life and Linda Green and Gene Sapp were elected new term members. In October of 2002, Jim Hudson, Peter Lowe, Martha Simms Rambo, and Mike Segrest were elected to their second terms on the Board.

In 2003, Hundley Batts, insurance company and radio station owner, retired Lt. General James Link, President of Teledyne Brown, and Jean Wessel Templeton, the local Burger King franchisee, were elected as term members to the Board, and Dr. Kendall Black and Russ Brown rotated off. Sid McDonald was elected as a life member of the Foundation Board.

In 2004, the Board would elect Colsa aerospace industrialist Frank Collazo and local attorney John Wynn as term members and Dr. Chan was elected a life member. That year Steve Monger rotated off the Board.

The Board would mourn the deaths of trustees Larry Durkee in 2003 and William T. Brooks, and the father of UAH Patrick Richardson in 2004.

In 2005 Clay Vandiver, President of the local Compass Bank; attorney William H. Johnson, Jr., who also serves on the Airport Authority, and would be added to the Trustees.

In 2006 Remigius Shatas, a UAH alumnus, local entrepreneur and cofounder of AVOCENT, and Phillip Bentley, Jr., owner of Bentley Motors and Chair of the Huntsville Hospital Board, would join the Trustees.

In 2007 Bhavani Kakani a local civic leader and UAH Alumnus; Kathy Chan, a UAH Alumnus, renowned artist and owner of Germano Jewelry Gallery; Roderick C. Steakley, a local attorney, and Frederiek Toney, Vice President of Ford Motor Company and a UAH alumnus; as well as Irma Tuder a local business woman and President and CEO of ASI, would be seated as members of the Trustees of the Foundation. Kathy Chan would be seated as a life member and Tony would be elected as a Trustee Emeritus.

Later in 2007 Linda Smith, a local civic leader, would be elected to be seated in 2008 and Mike Segrest who would be elected after being off of the board for several years would be re-elected for seating in 2008.

It was Richardson's dream of a university for his home town that helped lead to the creation of the University of Alabama in Huntsville and his business acumen that helped to start the UAH

Foundation and its predecessor organizations. Through his good work and that of the other founders of the Foundation and those who serve today, Huntsville is well positioned for the growth that is coming the area's way.

To all of those who have served on the Foundation Board, and to those who are serving today, the community owes much gratitude.

Appendix A

Alphabetical List of UAH Foundation
Board Members

Elected Trustees Serving in 2007

Batts, Sr., Hundley
Bendickson, Marcus J.
Bentley, Jr., Philip W.
Chan, Chia Hwa 'Tony'
Collazo, Frank J.
Green, Linda L.
Halsey, Jr., W. L.
Hendricks, John S.
Hudson, James R.
Johnston, Jr., Wm. H.
Jones, Raymond B.
Kakani, Bhavani
King, Olin B.
Link, (Ret.) LTG James M.
Lowe, Elizabeth
McDonald, Sidney L.
Moquin, Joseph
Nichols, Roy L.
Rambo, Martha Simms
Rowe, S. Dagnal
Sanders, Jr., W.F.
Sapp, Jr., A. Eugene
Segrest, James Michael
Shatas, Remigius
Smith, Linda
Steakley, Roderic G.
Templeton, Jean Wessel
Toney, Frederiek
Tuder, Irma L.
Vandiver, Clay
Wilkinson, Robert
Wynn, John R.

Former Elected Trustees

Bell, Robert K.
Black, J. Kendall
Blackwell, T. Alvin
Boone, Sr., Daniel C.
Brooks, William T.
Brown, Russell
Durkee, Larry
Hager, Robert W.
Heath, Robert H.
Horgen, Chris
Jones, Carl T.
Monger, J. Stephen
Moore, O. Howard
Nerren, Guy B.
Noojin, Jr., Frank K.
Noojin, Sr., F. Kenneth
Rhett, Harry M.
Richardson, Patrick
Salmon, Louis
Segrest, James Michael – (returned to active service)
Sexton, William Britt
Shaver, Sr., Charles E.
Smith, Mark C.
Spencer, Jr., Guy J.
Spragins, M. B.
Stevens, Jr., William H.
Thornton, Sr., Vance J.
Thrasher, Tom G.
Wilkinson, Robert

Appendix B

Founder Biographical Sketches

Robert Kirk "Buster" Bell

Robert K. "Buster" Bell was born in Tuscaloosa County in 1906.

Bell earned his Bachelors, Masters and LL.B. degrees from the University of Alabama. While attending the University he was a member of Kappa Sigma, Omicron Delta Kappa and Phi Delta Phi fraternities, Jasons, Farrah Order of Jurisprudence and Blue Key honorary societies. He served as national treasure of Omicron Delta Kappa.

Prior to establishing his Huntsville law practice in 1938 with Douglass Taylor and Judge Schuyler Richardson, Bell was assistant dean of men and a history professor at the University of Alabama from 1931 to 1938.

Bell entered the Alabama National Guard as a member of the Warrior Guards at Tuscaloosa. During World War II he served in Europe as assistant staff Judge Advocate, Headquarters European Theatre of Operations and Staff Judge Advocate, 1st Airborne Army with the rank of Major. He was awarded the Bronze Star medal, Oak Leaf Cluster and Meritorious Commendation medal. He retired from the National Guard as a lieutenant colonel.

Bell was active in legal, civic, and business circles. He was chairman of the board of directors (and a founder) of the American

National Bank and served as the County Attorney for Madison County from the 1940s until the time of his death. He was also a member of the Rotary Club.

Bell served as president of the Madison County Bar Association, the Alabama Junior Bar Association, the Huntsville Industrial Expansion Committee, the Huntsville/Madison County Chamber of Commerce, and the Alabama Wildlife Federation and was a past state commander of the Veterans of Foreign Wars. He was the State Bar Commissioner from the twenty-third Judicial Circuit from 1960-1963.

Bell married Carolyne Mason Pride in 1933. He died on December 31, 1966.

Daniel Carl Boone, Sr.

D. C. Boone died on May 9, 1981 at the age of 57. Mr. Boone was the founder and President of D. C. Boone Oil Inc. and Farms, he was a member of the board of directors of Peoples National Bank, the New Chamber of Commerce of Huntsville-Madison County, the foundation Boards of the University of Alabama in Huntsville and the University of Alabama. He was a member of the Episcopal Church of the Nativity. He was the 1958 recipient of the Chamber of commerce Distinguished Service Award.[157]

He was married to Una, and they had a son Daniel Carl Boone, Jr. and a daughter Sandra Donn.

A resolution was passed by Foundation Board on August 26, 1981 commemorating D. C. Boone's service to the University of Alabama Huntsville Foundation.

William L. Halsey, Jr.

William L. "Will" Halsey, Jr. was born in Huntsville September 8, 1920 in a house at 310 Lincoln St. His father, Will Sr. ran the family grocery business, which had been founded in 1879. His mother Elizabeth Lowry Halsey was the sister of Georgia Spragins, whose husband, M.B. Spragins, was also a founder of the UAH Foundation. He is a graduate of the Gulf Coast Military Academy.

Halsey was three weeks shy of graduating from the University of Alabama in 1942 when the Army called him to active duty. Alabama's chancellor, Dr. George Denny arranged for Halsey to get a deferment so he could graduate. "I had taken up flying while was at the University of Alabama, and I had also applied for the air Corps, well the air Corps subsequently got me. And I had about 72 hours flying time and then I had a little accident, and I got washed out. One week after I graduated, I was on active duty in Buzzards Bay Massachusetts. That was where they first had the engineering and amphibious command" Halsey said in an interview.

It happened that the day he had to leave for the service was the day he was to marry Jewel Fenandez, a co-ed from Tampa. Jewel went with him to Camp Edwards in Massachusetts, where they were going to live in the now-popular town of Buzzard's Bay, but Halsey said his wife wasn't going to have that (Buzzard's Bay) on her marriage license, so they were married in Wareham. He and Jewel would have three daughters over the years.

Halsey spent four years as an engineer in the Amphibian Command before being discharged with the rank of major in 1946. He returned to Huntsville to work in the family grocery business. In 1955 he became president and treasurer of the business.

Halsey was very active in the economic development of Huntsville serving as president of the Huntsville/Madison County Chamber of Commerce in 1953, and few years latter served as president of the Huntsville Madison County Industrial Expansion Committee/Industrial Development Association. He was a founding member of the Huntsville Industrial Development Board and served as vice chairman for many years.

He is also a former trustee of the Huntsville Hospital board of directors and has been active in the American Red Cross, YMCA and Boy Scouts and Girl Scouts of American fund-raising drives. He served a chairman of the Community Chest (now United Way) and a member of the NASA local advisory committee.

Halsey co-chaired the very successful effort to raise $750,000 to build the second building on the UAH campus. The effort actually netted over $880,000.

Halsey was active in a number of national and local industry associations serving as president of the Institutional Food Distributors of America, president of the Alabama Wholesale Grocer's Association. He is a past vice president of the Continental Organization of Distributor Enterprises as well as the U.S. Wholesale Grocers Association.

His local business affiliations include being a past director of First Alabama Bank, Huntsville, First Alabama Bancshares and a serving as a director of SCI Systems, Inc.

He was recognized as Outstanding Young Man of the Year in Huntsville in 1955 and received the Chamber of Commerce's Distinguished Citizen award in 1989. That same year he also received the American Defense Preparedness Association Distinguished Service Award. Halsey is a member of the local Army Advisory Committee and received the Outstanding Civilian Service Medal from Redstone Arsenal on three separate occasions.

Halsey also served on the appointed City School Board.

Carl Tannahill Jones

Carl Tannahill Jones was born December 12, 1908, in the Hurricane Creek community near Maysville, in Madison County, Alabama. Carl was the youngest of five sons and a daughter born to George Walter Jones and Elvonlena Moore Jones.

Carl's great grandfather, Isaac Criner, was one of Alabama's pioneer settlers having come to what is now Madison County, Alabama in 1802. The Jones family can trace its American lineage to the sixteenth century and are direct descendants of John Rolfe and Pocahontas.

Carl T. Jones grew up in Huntsville, Alabama where he graduated from Will-Taylor School. Like his brothers before him, he attended the University of Alabama in Tuscaloosa, Alabama where he graduated in May 1929 with a degree of B.S. in Civil Engineering. All of the Jones boys would earn degrees in civil engineering excepting brother Walter, who studied geology, eventually earning a PhD from Johns Hopkins University.

Following his graduation from the University, Carl briefly joined the family civil engineering firm G.W. Jones & Sons, Consulting Engineers, which his father had established in 1886 and where brothers Raymond, Howard, and Edwin also worked. The firm offered services in engineering, surveying, and abstracting. However, the firm faced hard times during the depression and Carl moved to Knoxville, Tennessee to work for the Forest Service.

He married the former Elizabeth Bryant on January 6, 1934 and they had three children, Raymond Bryant, Frances Elizabeth and Carolyn Tannahill.

In 1939 Carl returned to Huntsville and the family business. He and brother Edwin decided to diversify the Jones' family business to include farming. The two brothers purchased a 2,500 acre farm south of Huntsville, where Carl and his family would settle.

A short five months after Carl and his young family had moved onto the farm, the National Guard in Huntsville was mobilized and Carl was called to active duty. On January 27, 1941, the 151st Combat Engineers Alabama National Guard, was mobilized and set to Camp Shelby, Mississippi with a battalion under Carl's command. In July 1941 the battalion was sent to Kodiak, Alaska, becoming the first combat Engineer Battalion to go overseas in WWII. He was promoted to Colonel, Corps of Engineer and served as Chief of Staff of the Kiska Amphibious operations in the Aleutian Islands. Jones was named deputy chief of staff of the XIX Corps in Europe and participated with distinction in the Normandy landings and combat operations on the European front. At the end of the war he was an instructor in the amphibious section of the Army-Navy Staff

College, Washington, D.C. He returned to civilian status in March 1946.

His military decorations included the Legion of Merit, Bronze Star with Oak Leaf Cluster, Army Commendation Medal, Navy Commendation Medal, French Legion of Honor, Grade of Chevalier and French Croix de Guerre with Palm.

Returning to Huntsville after the war, Jones rejoined the family civil engineering firm and farming operations. The Jones firm served as Huntsville's city engineer from 1929 until 1960, a period of tremendous growth, much of which the Jones' firm had a hand in. Projects during this period included annexations that would expand the Huntsville city limits to more than 100 square miles beyond its 1950 four square mile boarder. G. W. Jones & Sons would be involved in surveying over 300 subdivisions, and providing civil engineering services for large sewer disposal and water filtration plants, and hundreds of local projects.

The farming operations were expanded to include considerable acreage for fescue seed growing and a processing facility. The family farmed approximately 3,000 acres of KY-31 fescue (some of which was leased from the Arsenal). The seed processing facility's capacity grew to 500,000 lbs of seed annually. The Jones' also purchased 400 head of heifers in the early 1950s. Farming operations would eventually grow to include cattle farms of approximately 10,000 acres.

Jones also became deeply involved in the economic development efforts of the community upon his return after World War II, joining the Board of Directors of the Huntsville Industrial Expansion Committee, the Huntsville/Madison County Chamber of Commerce. He helped to form several of the most important organizations that fueled Huntsville's incredible growth including Huntsville Industrial Associates, Huntsville Industrial Sites, the First National Bank of Huntsville, and the University of Alabama Huntsville Foundation. Jones was named to the Huntsville Industrial Development Board upon its creation in 1965.

Jones also found time to serve as President of the local Rotary Club, Newcomen Society, Professional Engineers Society, and the American Society of Civil Engineers.

Jones was honored with many awards including the Chamber's Distinguished Citizens Award in 1965, and Omicron Delta Kappa (honorary 1965). In 1983, Jones was posthumously inducted into the Alabama Business Hall of Fame.

Carl Tannahill Jones died while attending a University of Alabama – Ole Miss football game in Birmingham in 1967 at the age of 58. Shortly after his untimely death, the Huntsville

International Airport named it "Carl T. Jones Field" in recognition of his role in both developing the airport and leading the community's economic prosperity.

O. Howard Moore

O. Howard Moore was a native of Bell Factory, Alabama. He was born November 2, 1903 and died at the age of 74 on July 18, 1977. He was at the time of his death the tax assessor of Madison County a post he served from 1949 to his death. He served as deputy tax assessor from 1931 to 1949. He was the second longest tax assessor in the history of the county.

From the Huntsville Times Tuesday July 19, 1977:

" The residents of Madison County lost a dedicated public servant and an outstanding citizen Monday with the death of O. Howard Moore, tax assessor here for the past 28 years.

Mr. Moore's competence and knowledge were based on years of experience. Before being first elected tax assessor in 1949, Mr. Moore has served as deputy assessor for 14 years.

As tax assessor, he guided his office to the kind of balance between professionalism and courtesy that is so hard to find in government, yet so essential to the effective operation.

As a private citizen, Mr. Moore was one of many who were instrumental in seeing Huntsville and Madison County through the growth years if the 1950s and 1960s. He was active in encouraging industrial development, and his membership in the University of Alabama in Huntsville Foundation indicated his sincere interest in providing education opportunities to all county residents."[158]

F. Kenneth Noojin, Sr.

F. Kenneth Noojin Sr. was a longtime Huntsville resident, born in 1918. He was active in hardware, lumber and real estate business after service as an officer in the Navy in the Pacific during WWII.

He was one of the first developers of subdivisions and apartments in post-war Huntsville and surrounding areas and was also the principal developer of Parkway City Shopping Center, Huntsville's first such facility.

Noojin was active in community and business groups. He had served as president of the Madison County Community Chest, president of the Huntsville Rotary Club and district governor of Rotary International, president of the Civic Club Council, president of the Huntsville Industrial Expansion Committee, president of the UMCA board, president of the Huntsville Country Club, a director of the Alabama Retail Hardware Association, vice president of the University of Alabama Alumni Association and a director of the University of Alabama Huntsville Foundation.

He was a member of First United Methodist Church and a past member of the Board of Stewards.

Harry Moore Rhett, Jr.

Harry M. Rhett, Jr. was born March 3, 1912, in Huntsville, Alabama, into a prominent local family of position and privilege.

Rhett received his grade school education at the Culver Military Academy, his Bachelors degree from Washington and Lee University and Masters Degree in Business Administration from Harvard Business School.

He served as an officer in WWII and became the youngest military installation commander in the U.S. Army before going overseas to serve in North Africa and Italy. He completed his wartime service with the rank of Major.

Upon his return to Huntsville Rhett joined his family's firm, the Rison Banking Company. The firm merged with National Bank of Huntsville, later becoming First Alabama Bank.

Rhett was well known as a gentleman farmer and real estate manager. He and his firm developed Huntsville's Parkway City Mall.

Rhett devoted a tremendous amount of time to public service, including serving as chairman of the Gas and Water Utility boards and the Madison County Board of Registrars.

221

He was a founder of Randolph School and served as chairman of its board of trustees for 15 years. He was the founding chairman of the Huntsville Hospital Foundation and the Huntsville Museum of Art Foundation.

He served as treasurer of the UAH Foundation and was a member of the advisory committee of the Huntsville-Madison County Botanical Garden.

He as a past president of the Huntsville Rotary Club, Huntsville Industrial Expansion Committee, the Twickenham Historic Preservation District and the Huntsville/Madison County Chamber of Commerce.

Rhett also served as the Senior Warden of the Episcopal Church of the Nativity.

Rhett was an avid equestrian and founded the Mooreland Hunt and served as master of foxhounds. He received the Humanitarian award from the North East branch of the Alabama Chapter of the Arthritis Foundation.

Rhett and his wife had four children, two daughters and two sons. He died February 3, 1996, at the age of 83.

Patrick W. Richardson

Patrick W. Richardson was born in Huntsville, Alabama in 1925 and graduated from local public schools.

In 1943 he was nominated by his father's law partner, U.S. Senator John Sparkman, to attend the U.S. Army Military Academy in West Point, New York. While a freshman "plebe" at the Academy, he was hit hard in the back of the neck by an errant foul ball from an adjoining field during a softball game. Richardson subsequently suffered from a couple of fainting spells. Following a concerned call from Sen. Sparkman, doctors at Walter Reed Hospital discovered the ball had damaged a nerve bundle in Richardson's neck, causing low blood pressure and a sluggish pulse, ending his hopes for a military career.

Richardson returned to Huntsville and then enrolled at the University of Alabama, applying his military disability benefits to pay his way through school. He earned a degree in economics and then entered law school in Tuscaloosa. While in law school he taught economics as a graduate fellow. It was about this time in 1946, while he was still a law student, that he began pitching the idea of locating a university extension office in Huntsville. Those efforts were eventually successful and Richardson was hired as one of the first instructors at the fledgling university center following his graduation from law school.

A leader in the industrial development efforts of the community, Richardson would become involved with the Huntsville Industrial Expansion Committee. He served as the first chairman of the UAH Foundation and its predecessor organizations from 1962 to 1973. He received a UAH Honorary Doctor of Laws degree in 1976. He was also the recipient of the UAH President's Medal, and the Distinguished Civic Service Award of the UAH Alumni Association.

He was instrumental in establishing Randolph School, and was a recipient of many civic awards including the James Record Humanitarian Award, the John Sparkman Award of Madison County and the UA Alumni Association Award.

Richardson and his first wife, Martha (Simms Rambo) had two sons, Dick and Jim.

Patrick Richardson died November 14, 2004. Like several other Foundation members who had passed before him, his family asked that, in lieu of flowers, that memorial gifts be made to the Patrick W. Richardson Memorial Scholarship Fund at the University of Alabama Huntsville Foundation. Donation cards were made available at the memorial service.

Charles Shaver, Sr.

Charles E. Shaver was born in Huntsville on December 6, 1907. He attended public schools in Huntsville and received both his bachelor's and law degree from Vanderbilt University.

His legal scholarship was recognized by election to the order of the Coif and at graduation from the law school received the Founders Medal.

Shaver was admitted to the Alabama Bar and the Tennessee Bar in 1931. He served as president of the Huntsville-Madison County Bar Association and was on the Board of Commissioners for the Alabama Bar Association from 1966 through 1972. He was a founding partner in the Huntsville law firm of Lanier, Ford, Shaver and Payne.

Shaver was a member of the Alabama House of Representatives from 1935 to 1939 and an Alabama State Senator from 1939 to 1947. While in the Legislature, he served on the Code Committee that revised the Alabama Code of 1923 and wrote the Alabama Code of 1940 that consist of all statutory laws enacted by the State Legislature.

The Honorable Chauncey Sparks, Governor of Alabama, offered Shaver a vacant Madison County Circuit judgeship in 1944, which he declined.

Shaver was instrumental in guiding numerous gifts to the University of Alabama in Huntsville through the Foundation. He served on numerous University of Alabama in Huntsville citizen advisory committees including the University of Alabama in Huntsville Associates, the President's Advisory Council, and he served on a special committee appointed by the Board of Trustees to recommend the selection of the first and second President of UAH.

For many years he served as a member of the Board of Directors of the First Alabama Bank of Huntsville (formerly the Henderson National Band), Huntsville Coca-Cola Bottling Company and for twenty years a director of the Alabama Safety Council. He also served as president of the Huntsville Kiwanis Club, the Acme Club, a Charter member and past Exalted Ruler of the Elks Club, and active in the Masonic Lodge. He was a Shriner and a trustee of the Presbyterian Home for Children.

Shaver was active in the organizations that brought economic growth to the region including the Huntsville/Madison County Chamber of Commerce and the Huntsville-Madison County Industrial Development Association for more than a quarter century. He was recognized for his community service with the Chamber's

Distinguished Citizen Award in 1981. He was also a member of the Huntsville Industrial Development Board at the time of its inception in 1965.

Shaver was also involved in a number of youth organizations including the Boy Scouts of America serving as an officer in the county and regional boards. He helped organize the Huntsville Boys Club in 1955 and served as a board member through the 1980s.

Shaver served as a trustee at the First Presbyterian Church here and was a former board member of the Church's Home for Children, based in Talladega.

He was married to the former Sarah Moorman of Huntsville and they had two sons and one daughter. He died Jan. 10, 1993.

Marion Beirne Spragins

Marion Beirne Spragins was born in Huntsville on Oct. 9, 1892 to the Honorable Robert Elias and Susan Patton (Echols) Spragins. Robert Spragins, like his father before him, served as president of First National Bank, in Huntsville. Robert Spragins was a state senator and a delegate to the Alabama constitutional convention in 1901.

Spragins attended private schools and graduated from St. Luke's School in Wayne, Pennsylvania in 1910. He earned his A.B degree from the University of Alabama, in 1914, where he was a member of the Phi Delta Theta fraternity.

During the summer of 1913, he was employed as a collector by the First National Bank of Huntsville and after graduating from college, became a bookkeeper and later assistance cashier and discount clerk for the bank. In May 1917 he enlisted for service in the World War I, and on May 6, entered the Officers' Training Camp, at Ft. Oglethorpe, Ga. and was commissioned a 1st lieut. in the Field Artillery 31st division. In December 1917, he was sent to Ft. Sill, Oklahoma for special training as an Artillery observer with the Aviation Corps following which he returned to the 31st division at Camp Wheeler. He served overseas for six months, remaining in France until after the Armistice was signed. He was honorably discharged on January 14, 1919.

Returning to Huntsville following the war, he went to work again at the First National Bank, leaving shortly thereafter to become the bookkeeper for the Huntsville Ice & Coal Company. He was made general manager of that company. In 1933, in the midst of the Great Depression, he was named executive vice president of the First National Bank and following his father's death in 1935, was made president January 1, 1936.

Spragins was a director of the Lincoln Mills of Alabama, the Huntsville Ice & Coal Company, the Fletcher Mills, Inc. and the Farmers Warehouse Company. He also owned several farms around Madison County.

Spragins was a member of the Birmingham Branch of the Federal Reserve Bank of Atlanta, chairman of the Alabama Bankers Association Legislation Committee and a member of the Advisory Committee to the U.S. Senate Banking and Currency Committee. From 1946 – 1967, Spragins served as a member of the Third Army Advisory Committee, and for his service received the Outstanding Civilian Service Award for his contributions to the liaison between the Army and the citizenry.

He was President/Chairman of the Board for the Chamber of Commerce in 1946. In 1963 he was awarded the Huntsville Distinguished Citizens Award by the Huntsville Madison County

Chamber of Commerce. Spragins was posthumously inducted into the Alabama Business Hall of Fame in November of 1977.

On April 26, 1920 he married Huntsville native Georgia Lowry and they had one daughter and three sons. He died in 1973, leaving a significant amount of property to the University of Alabama Foundation.

Vance J. Thornton

Vance J. Thornton was born on May 20, 1916 in Fayetteville, Tennessee. His family moved to Huntsville when he was just 16 months old and he graduated from Huntsville High School.

Thornton served in WWII in the 80th Infantry Division, part of Gen. Patton's Third Army and earned a purple heart for wounds received in combat and a bronze star.

For a number of years, he worked with the First National Bank of Huntsville and established the small loan office of the bank after the war. He was an assistant national bank examiner for three years, working out of Atlanta.

He was in the banking, insurance and real estate business in Huntsville for the 14 years preceding his death, as senior partner in the real estate firm of Thornton and Thornton. He was also a member of the board of directors of the First Federal Savings and Loan Association of Huntsville since 1952. He was one of the owners of the Kings Inn Motor Hotel.

At the time of his death, Mr. Thornton was president of Huntsville Industrial Sites, a member of the Industrial Development Board of the city of Huntsville, vice president of the University of

Alabama Huntsville Foundation and treasurer of the Huntsville Industrial Expansion Committee.

Thornton was a Shriner, active in the American Legion, V.F.W., Rotary, D.A.V, and Chairman of the Red Cross. He served as a trustee for Huntsville Hospital and Cripple Children's Association.

He was a member and elder of the First Presbyterian Church of Huntsville.

He was elected to three terms on the Huntsville City Council in beginning in 1948 and ending as president of the council.

Thornton died in his sleep December 12, 1965 at the age of 49.

An editorial in the December 14, 1965 issue of the *Huntsville Times* noted with great sadness the sudden passing of this great community leader. It said "The success of the man had its basis in infectious enthusiasm. But additionally it had to be rooted in his ability as a good planner and organizer. And this enthusiasm and ability were re-enforced by persistence – he was not one to let a mission, once started, go unfulfilled or be put aside in a quest for another goal."

Tom Goodman Thrasher

Tom G. Thrasher was born in Wetumpka, Alabama on August 4, 1916 to Mae Goodman Thrasher and Eugene Wilson Thrasher, a deputy sheriff in Elmore County, Al. Tom's father died when he was 9 months old and soon thereafter his mother moved the family, which included Tom's older brother and sister to Birmingham in 1917. There Tom's mother took a job teaching at Inglenook Grammar School in Jefferson County, a position she would hold for the next 40 years.

Tom graduated from Phillips High School in Birmingham in 1932. He worked three years prior to enrolling in the mechanical engineering program at the University of Alabama in Tuscaloosa in 1935.

In 1939 Tom was a 2nd Lt. with the Corps of Engineers with the Civilian Conservation Crops as a Jr. Officer in a CCC camp at Shuqualah, Mississippi where he worked from March thru September of 1939. He was then given a job as a civilian officer with a civil service rating of CAF2. One month later he was assigned command of a CCC company at Tishomingo, Mississippi with a civil service rating of CAF 7.

While in the CCC he met Dorothy Write of Belmont, Mississippi and they married in September of 1940.

A few months before the Japanese bombed Pearl Harbor; Thrasher was called into active duty with the Army in August of 1941 and received a commission as a 2nd Lt in the Ordnance Corps. Thrasher would remain in the Northern African and European theaters from October 1942, until December of 1945, at which time he returned stateside and was discharged with the rank of Lt. Colonel in March of 1946.

Following his discharge he returned to Birmingham where he was encouraged by his family to look into finding an oil distributorship.

"I went to the Shell Oil Distributor and asked a Mr. Herrell there is he knew of anything." Thrasher said. "I didn't have any civilian clothes and was still dressed in my Army Uniform. He said he didn't know of a thing, so I was about to leave when I asked if he knew David Herrell.[1]

"David had been a friend of mine at Phillips High School. Well, he (the oil company Herrell) wheeled around and said David was his brother and how did I know him. When I told him he said for me to sit down, he might know of something in Huntsville that I'd be interested in."

In May of 1946 Thrasher bought a Guntersville man's half interest in one service station in Huntsville and took over the lease on another, using money Dorothy Thrasher had saved while Tom was serving in WWII. Thrasher opened Thrasher Oil Co. with the two stations he owned and a warehouse leased from Shell.

"I went from a Lt. Col. to a truck driver," he said in a 1998 interview. It was a change he never regretted.

When the Korean War broke out, Thrasher was ordered back to active duty from May of 1951 until Oct. of 1952, a total of 17 months, 16 of which were served at Redstone Arsenal as the Executive Officer. He was able to keep the oil business running by hiring a disabled veteran.

Thrasher got his start in civic affairs the same year that he completed his tour of active duty on Redstone Arsenal due in part to Vance Thornton, a close friend who was chairman of the Huntsville City Council. Thrasher served on the Huntsville City School Board from 1952 – 1961 and was president of the board for two years.

Previously, Thrasher had worked with Huntsville Attorney Pat Richardson to help start the University of Alabama Extension Center.

Thrasher was also a member of the Army Community Relations Committee, a civic support organization formed to support the Arsenal.

His involvement in the economic development of Huntsville was extensive. He was selected as a member of the Huntsville Industrial Expansion Committee Board of Directors first in 1958 and served as chairman in 1964-1965. He was a director of the Huntsville Industrial Associates, and Huntsville Madison County Chamber of Commerce. He was chairman of the Huntsville Medical Clinic Board, was a member of the NASA local advisory committee, vice chairman of the Von Braun Civic Center feasibility study board and the civic center's construction and operating board and chairman of its board of control. He was also chairman of the Huntsville Convention and Visitor Bureau board. He was among the first people appointed to serve on the Industrial Development Board in 1965, a post he held until 1976, serving as Chairman.

His other leadership positions included a 1961 appointment by President Kennedy to the National USO Board, 1958 appointment to the U.S. Army Civilian Advisory Committee, Third Army Area Headquarters, Atlanta Georgia, Board of Directors, Alabama Chamber of Commerce 1962-the 1980s, director-at-large for the Alabama Oil Jobbers Association.

He was a president of the Shriners, the Kiwanis Club, March of dimes, Madison County Oil Distributors Association, Tennessee Valley Association of the U.S. Army,

In 1976 Thrasher was awarded an honorary Doctor of Humanities degree by UAH. Citing his many years of public service at that commencement ceremony, the University observed "We have here a talented individual who has chosen to share his energies with his fellow man. The University is fortunate indeed to have such a friend."[1]

In 1978, Thrasher personally helped to get the UAH hockey program off the ground with a $5,000 personal donation to cover the costs of the uniforms according to former team coach Joe Ritch "It was totally unsolicited and he took no credit for the contribution." "I give him a great deal of credit for us being able to get off the ground."

Thrasher was the father of four daughters. He died in December of 1999.

INDEX

Lowe Industrial Park, *113*

M

Madison County Chase Industrial Park. *See* Chase Industrial Park

Madison Hall, 78, 83, 91

Mahoney
  George, *ix, 10, 11, 21, 22, 23, 24, 25, 31*

Marietta Tool & Die. *See* Brown Engineering

Marshall Space Flight Center, *47, 48, 50, 59, 61, 63*, 111, *157*

Martin Industrial Park, *113*

Mason
  Phillip, *83*
  W. O., *24*

Master Plan, *180, 182*

Matheny
  Herschel, *115*

Mathews
  Dean Y., *49*

Matthews
  F. David, *121*

McDonald
  Sid, *193, 194*

McElroy
  Neil, *38*

McGlathery
  David M., *77*

McGregor
  Edward, *24*

McNaron
  Abner C., *75*

Medaris
  John Bruce, *39, 41*

Medlock
  James, *115, 151*

Mella
  Lorenzo A., *17*

Michel
  Josef, *17*

Miller
  James C., *17*

Mills
  Walter, *27*

Mitchell
  Ed, *172, 249*

Mock
  C. J., *24*

Monger
  Steve, *173, 192, 193, 194*

Monroe
  H. E., *24, 26*

Moore
  O. Howard, *45, 60, 69, 84, 123, 140*

Moquin
  Joseph, *47, 48, 49, 139, 140, 155, 156*

Morgan
  Derald, *170, 176, 177, 178, 179, 180, 181*

Morton
  John, *3, 4, 5, 6, 26, 57*

Morton Hall, *57, 120*

Mosley
  Mickey, *151*

N

NASA, *40, 43, 54, 63, 93*, 111, *164, 165*

Nelson
  Harvey D., 4, 6, 26

Nerren
  Guy, *32, 43, 44, 45, 46, 57, 59, 60, 65, 69, 76, 84, 87, 88, 89, 123, 138, 142, 144, 151, 154, 155, 172*

Nichols
  Roy, *173, 192, 194*

Noble
  Percy, *24*

Noojin
  Frank, *194*
  Kenneth, *ix, 31, 32, 60, 84, 127, 138*

North Campus Residence Hall, *182, 189*

North Campus Residence Hall II, *189*

Northrop, *48, 65*

O

Ordnance Rocket Center, *15*

P

Padulo
  Louis, *153, 154, 155, 158*

245

FOOTNOTES

1. William Joseph Stubno Jr., educational data in master's thesis, "The Impact of the von Braun Board of Directors on the American Space Program," University of Alabama in Huntsville, 1980.

2. UAH Alumni News, summer 2001, Vol. 1 No. 2

3. UAH Magazine, Winter 1990, Cheri Shipper, "What will UAH be by the year 2020 A.D.?"

4. The Huntsville Times, January 5, 1975, Don Eddins, "University of Alabama in Huntsville Looks Back on Its First 25 Years" p. 13

5. The University of Alabama in Huntsville – A History" James E. Ferguson III, Spring 1975, p. 7

6. L.H. Pinkston to Huntsville Chamber of Commerce, Huntsville, Alabama, June 16, 1947

7. UAH Alumni News, summer 2001, Vol. 1 No. 2, p. 9

8. Ibid., p. 5

9. Ibid., p. 9

10. Ibid., p. 9

11. University of Alabama Extension News Bulletin, Vol. 7, No. 8, University of Alabama Feb., 1950

12. UAH Alumni News, summer 2001 p. 9

13. L.H. Pinkston to Mr. P.W. Peeler, Lincoln Mills of Alabama, Huntsville, AL, June 14, 1949

14. The Huntsville Times, September 22, 1949, "January Date Is Indicated on New Center," p. 1

15. Pat Richardson to Dr. John M. Gallalee, President, University of Alabama, Sept. 21, 1949

16. The Huntsville Times, November 14, 1949, p. 1, "Center Hinges on Attendance At Conference"

17. The Huntsville Times, July 10, 1963, "Arsenal Born 22 Years Ago" by Bob Ward.

18. A Report on Madison County, Its History, Operations and Finances, December 13, 1951, James R. Record, County Auditor, p. 34

19. Redstone Arsenal, by Dr. Kaylene Hughes

20. The Impact of Space Age Spending on the Economy of Huntsville, Alabama by Thomas Franklin Morring, Master of Science Thesis at MIT, 1964, (unpublished manuscript)

21. America and Germany Evolution of a Friendship, "German Rocketeers Find a New Home in Huntsville" by Ernst Stuhlinger, September 21, 1995, p. 6

22. Dr. Space, the Life of Wernher von Braun, Bob Ward, 2005, Naval Institute Press, p. 74

23. Biography of Carl T. Jones, Alabama Business Hall of Fame Inductee, Program 1983

24. Interview with J.E. "Ed" Mitchell, Jr., February 10, 2006

25. Sesquicentennial 1805-1955 – Huntsville, Alabama, Commemorative Album, chapter nine

26. 75 Years of Service, A History of the Huntsville Rotary Club by Bill Easterling, 1992, p. 40

27. Huntsville, Alabama – Huntsville has what it takes, p. 17, published by the Huntsville Industrial Expansion Committee (undated-1946-47)

28. Huntsville and the Space Program: Part One: The Beginnings through 1960, Alabama Heritage magazine, Mike Wright, Spring 1998, p. 41

29. University of Alabama Extension News Bulletin, Vol. 7, No. 8 University of Alabama February, 1950

30. UAH History, unpublished manuscript, James Record, Huntsville Public Library, local archives collection.

31. UAH Alumni News, summer 2001, Vol. 1, No. 2, p. 10

32. UAH History unpublished manuscript, James Record, Huntsville Public Library, local archives collection.

33. 50 years of Rocketry and Space – Huntsville, Alabama, NASA MSFC Retirees Association, 2002

34. Ibid.

35. The Huntsville Times, May 13, 1953.

36. History of University of Alabama Huntsville Foundation, undated, Patrick Richardson

37. The University of Alabama Huntsville Foundation, A History, a speech delivered by Louis Salmon to the Huntsville Rotary Club on September 30, 1992.

38. Ibid.

39. Interview with Guy Nerren, April 26, 2005

40. Sesquicentennial 1805-1955 – Huntsville, Alabama, Commemorative Album, Chapter nine

41. 50 Years of Rockets and Space Craft, 2002, NASA-MSFC Retiree Association, p. 61

42. Rocket City USA – From Huntsville, Alabama to the Moon, Erik Bergaust, MacMillan Company, 1963, p. 80

43. Population Huntsville – Madison County, A report based on the Special Census of September 22, 1964 prepared by the Huntsville City Planning Commission in March 1965, p. 22

44. Biography of Carl T. Jones, Alabama Business Hall of Fame Inductee, Program 1983

45. The Huntsville Times, June 6, 1954

46. UAH Alumni News summer 2001, Vol. 1, No. 2, p. 11

47. UAH History, by James Record, Huntsville Public Library, local archives collection.

48. The Huntsville Times, August 8, 1958

49. Time magazine cover story, "Missileman von Braun," February 17, 1958

50. UAH Alumni News summer 2001, Vol. 1 No. 2, p. 12

51. The Impact of Space Age Spending on the Economy of Huntsville by Thomas Franklin Morring, Master's Thesis MIT, 1964, p.19 – (unpublished manuscript)

52. Ibid.,

53. Chamber of Commerce Initiatives article "Huntsville's Research Park Joe Moquin's 20/20 Site," February 2005

54. Ibid., p. 10

55. Ibid., p. 10

56. Interview with W.L. "Will" Halsey, Jr. March 21, 2005

57. The University of Alabama in Huntsville – A History by James E. Ferguson III, Spring 1975, p. 33

58. Research Institute promotional materials developed by the HIEC, 1963.

59. The University of Alabama in Huntsville – A History by James E. Ferguson III, Spring 1975, p. 33

60. Interview with Joe Moquin, May 2005

61. Remarks by Dr. Wernher von Braun, Director, George C. Marshall Space Flight Center to a Joint Session of the Alabama Legislature, Montgomery, Alabama, June 20, 1961

62. Interview with Will Halsey, March 21, 2005

63. "History of the Graduate Program," Charles Dodson, Huntsville, 1969, p. 7 (unpublished manuscript)

64. Interview with David Johnson

65. Louis Salmon, speech to the Huntsville Rotary Club, September 30, 1992

66. UAH Alumni News, Summer 2001, Vol.1 No. 2, interview with Patrick Richardson

67. Louis Salmon, speech to the Huntsville Rotary Club, September 30, 1992

68. Interview with Guy Nerren April 26, 2005

69. Research Sites Foundation Articles of Incorporation (Book 11, Page 723 State of Alabama, Madison County), October 24, 1962, In the Probate Court.

70. History of University of Alabama Huntsville Foundation, Pat Richardson, undated & unpublished manuscript

71. Louis Salmon, speech to the Huntsville Rotary Club, September 30, 1992

72. The Impact of Space Age Spending on the Economy of Huntsville by Thomas Franklin Morring, Master's Thesis MIT, 1964, p.14 – (unpublished manuscript)

73. "Sales Management Magazine Quarterly Retail Sales Forecast," published in The Huntsville Times, January 12, 1964

74. The Impact of Space Age Spending on the Economy of Huntsville by Thomas Franklin Morring, Master's Thesis MIT, 1964, p.14 – (unpublished manuscript)

75. "Population Huntsville – Madison County," A report based on the Special Census of September 22, 1964, prepared by Huntsville City Planning Commission March 1965

76. Huntsville, Ala. "Where Space Begins…and Never Ends," Community promotional material published by The Huntsville Times, Revised August 1, 1963

77. City of Huntsville Report, 1964, Huntsville Library Archives Collection

78. Interview with Guy Nerren, April 26, 2005

79. Frank Morring

80. City of Huntsville Report, 1964, Huntsville Library Archives Collection

81. Minutes, Board of Directors Meeting, Huntsville Industrial Sites, Inc., February 19, 1964.

82. Minutes, Board of Directors Meeting, Huntsville Industrial Sites, Inc., March, 1964.

83. Interview with David Johnston, 2005

84. Louis Salmon, Speech to the Huntsville Rotary Club, September 30, 1992

85. Louis Salmon, Speech to the Huntsville Rotary Club, September 30, 1992

86. Minutes of the UAH Foundation, March 28, 1968

87. Louis Salmon, Speech to the Huntsville Rotary Club, September 30, 1992

88. Research Park Advisory Board minutes, September 1, 1965, UAH special archives

89. Frank Morring p. 21

90. Frank Morring p. 21

91. Huntsville Industrial Development Board records located at the Huntsville Madison County Chamber of Commerce

92. The University of Alabama in Huntsville – A History James E. Ferguson III, Spring 1975, p. 36

93. Ibid., p. 38

94. UAH Alumni News Summer 2001, Vol. 1 No. 2, p. 12

95. Ibid., p. 12

96. Interview with W.L. "Will" Halsey, Jr., March 21, 2005

97. An Analysis of Aerospace/Defense Economic Impact and Industrial Development Opportunities in Huntsville, Alabama, Report prepared by the Office of Economic Adjustment Office of the Assistant Secretary of Defense (Installations and Logistics), The Pentagon, Washington DC 20301, November 1974

98. New York Times, September 24, 1967, p. 80

99. U.S. News & World Report magazine, October 14, 1968

100. Interview with Martha Simms Rambo, 2005

101. Analysis of Aerospace/Defense Economic Impact and Industrial Development Opportunities in Huntsville, Alabama, Report prepared by the Office of Economic Adjustment Office of the Assistant Secretary of Defense (Installations and Logistics), The Pentagon, Washington DC 20301, November 1974

102. OEA study

103. Ibid

104. Interview with David Johnston, 2005

105. interview with Guy Nerren, April 26, 2005

106. Ibid.

107. UAH Alumni News summer 2001, Vol. 1 No. 2, p. 13

108. UAH Foundation minutes July 13, 1967

109. UAH Alumni News summer 2001, Vol. 1 No. 2, p. 14

110. Fortune Magazine, 1967

111. Dr. Benjamin Graves, address to the Huntsville Rotary Club, 1970

112. Huntsville Business Trends, Huntsville/Madison County Chamber of Commerce, May 1974, Pg. 7

113. An Analysis of Aerospace / Defense Economic Impact and Industrial Development Opportunities in Huntsville, AL, Office of Economic Adjustment, Office of the Assistant Secretary of Defense, November 1974

114. Huntsville Business Trends, Huntsville/Madison County Chamber of Commerce, May 1974, Pg. 8

115. Ibid., Pg. 6

116. Fantus economic development analysis for Huntsville, Alabama, 1960, Huntsville Industrial Expansion Committee

117. OEA study

118. Louis Salmon, Rotary Club speech, September 30, 1992.

119. Ibid.

120. OEA report.

121. Huntsville/Madison County Industrial Directory 1977-78, compiled and published by the Huntsville/Madison County Industrial Development Association

122. The Honorable Robert T. Wilson, Estimated replacement value – appropriation request support documents February 8, 1971

123. UAH Foundation Board minutes, December 31, 1974 "Foundation votes to pay off lease on "Kroger property" of $21,550 when the University purchases same for $520,000 from Harry Rhett." .

124. UAH Alumni News, Summer 2001, Vol. 1 No. 2,, Pg 14

125. Interview with Dr. Benjamin Graves, April 12, 2005

126. Ibid.

127. UAH Foundation minutes

128. Interview with Dr. Benjamin Graves, April 12, 2005

129. UAH Foundation minutes

130. Dividend$, College of Administrative Science, UAH, Fall 1999/Winter 2000, pg. 7

131. Dr. Benjamin Graves, College of Administrative Science, UAH, "Dividend$" Fall 1999/Winter 2000, pg 7.

132. UAH Alumni News, Summer 2001, Vol. 1 No. 2,, Pg 14

133. Ibid

134. Interview with Dr. Graves, April 12, 2005

135. UAH Alumni News, Summer 2001, Vol. 1 No. 2,, Pg 14

136. UAH Alumni News, Summer 2001, Vol. 1 No. 2, Pg 15

137. Interview with Martha Simms Rambo, April 11, 2005

138. Interview with Dr. Graves, May, 2005

139. UAH Alumni News, Summer 2001, Pg. 17

140. UAH Foundation Minutes, November 11, 1977

141. Interview with Dr. John C. Wright, September 29, 2005

142. Ibid.

143. Interview with Guy Nerren, April 26, 2005

144. A Special Report UAH – 1969 – 1979, "The University of Alabama Huntsville Foundation"

145. Interview with W.F. Sanders

146. Huntsville/Madison County Chamber of Commerce – Cummings Research Park – Internet materials

147. The Huntsville Times, October 6, 1982

148. The University of Alabama Huntsville Foundation, A History, by Jerry Quick, based on a speech to the Huntsville Rotary Club, September 1992.

149. Interview with Guy Nerren April 26, 2005

150. Interview with Dr. Frank Franz October 10, 2005

151. Interview with Brian Hilson, August 1, 2007

152. Interview with Sara James Graves, July 30, 2007

153. UAH Foundation minutes, January 7, 1993

154. The Huntsville Times, June 18, 1999, pg. C 1, by Pat Newcomb

155. University of Alabama Huntsville Foundation, Annual Report 1999, inside cover.

156. The Huntsville Times June 14, 2003, page B 1, by Kenneth Kesner

157. The Huntsville Times May 10, 1981, pages A 1 and May 11, 1981

158. The Huntsville Times, July 19, 1977 Editorial Page

Printed in the United States
136223LV00002B/162/P

9 781438 944685